I0798547

MANGUS THE MOTHERF*CKER

and Other Plays

MANGUS THE MOTHERF*CKER

and Other Plays

MURRAY MEDNICK

PADUA PLAYWRIGHTS PRODUCTION

Padua Playwrights Press

First Edition 2025

10 9 8 7 6 5 4 3 2 1

Produced by Sideshow Media LLC, Brooklyn NY

Editorial director and producer: Dan Tucker
Cover design: Brian McWilliams
Supervising Padua editor: Guy Zimmerman
Layout: Corinda Cook

Printed in the United States of America

Distributed in the United States and Canada by Theatre Communications Group, 520 Eighth Avenue, 24th Floor, New York, NY 10018-4156

CONTENTS

SCENES FROM A VANISHED WORLD

Guy Zimmerman

Back when the East Village was a separate zone of art and resistance, before the rents went up and the financial crisis of the 1970s cratered arts funding city-wide, you could meet militant hipsters roaming around who were authentic members of The Motherfuckers (also known as *Up Against the Wall, Motherfucker!*), serious figures such as Amiri Baraka and the poets Ben Morea and Dan Georgakas, who did things like cut the fences at Woodstock to let hundreds in for free, and fling garbage at the U.S. Secretary of State to protest the war in Vietnam. As Mangus puts it in the play: "We were Anarchists, we meant business. The Motherfuckers. Upending the System as much as we could. There was a War on." Maybe one of these Motherfuckers was named Mangus and Murray knew him; more likely, Murray imagined himself in the role just for the fun of it, positioning Mangus with his wife Lark at the far end of the galaxy astride the event horizon of a black hole.

Toward the end of his run as the artistic director of Theater Genesis, Murray mounted a version of *Mangus* titled *Black Hole in Space* but the production didn't fly. Murray had written much of *Black Hole* while coming down off of methadone in the Yucatan, an arduous ordeal. This had been Murray's third trip to Mexico and he drew on his experience of that foreign milieu. The play invoked the temples and the ruins of ancient Mayans and Aztecs, and the sacrificial violence of those distant cultures, figures in the action. *Black Hole in*

Space included a film component and some autobiographical material Murray came to dislike, but also "had a dark center to it having to do with the murder." Murray liked the basic premise of *Black Hole* and some of the speeches could also be salvaged, and so the title play of this new collection *Mangus the Motherfucker* was born.

Mangus has fun with the science fiction genre and the theory of black holes. The density of a collapsed star bending gravity creates an altered, anarchic case of physical reality to work with. As noted above, *Mangus* takes place within the black hole's event horizon, giving Mangus and Lark freedom from the limitations of the normative. The conceit acts as a springboard for Murray to mess around with space and time, exploring the remarkable mobility of the stage. The couple are haunted by a priest wearing a jaguar mask, and a Peter Lorre character named Mr. Zinc reporting on apocalyptic events. Thematically, Murray was interested also in the darkness of gullibility and delusion. Over the course of the play the young man Dave comes into possession of an Aztec diagram linked to the practice of sacrifice, and he puts it into action by murdering his parents, a transference to which Mangus and Lark remain oblivious. They have kids at home and get glimpses of them, shifting back to observe their former ordinary lines. David is on the loose and he tells them he was inspired by the Mexican slaughter.

Mangus, like many of Murray's plays, combines weighty issues with a weightless delivery, the language raising everything up toward the vertical sublime. The image of a black hole is drenched in irony—the event horizon replicating the introversion of the kind of rampant drug abuse that had begun to darken the countercultural project as the 1970s came on. There are interesting resonances between *Black Hole in Space* and Murray's final Genesis play, *Are You Lookin'*, which had a successful run in New York and was then re-mounted in Los Angeles with Ed Harris in the lead role. The topic of drug addiction that is implicit in *Black Hole* became explicit in *Lookin'*; in *Mangus* these resonances are more humorous but still detectable. Generational politics unfold amid the sci-fi touches and comedic asides as Mangus and Lark move back and forth between past and future.

It's become difficult to imagine the episode of US cultural history known as the '60s except as a marketing brand involving love beads, long hair and bell bottoms. The overt danger of the war that raged in Vietnam fueled an urgent sense of radical possibility, if only the correct revolutionary steps could be made. At the far edge today of the right-wing counter-revolution that began with Reagan, it's refreshing to touch base with that spirit of resistance. Read through Murray's *Mangus the Motherfucker* and you'll feel a bracing draft from that more spacious time, when sobering truths could still be confronted directly, in the name of self-respect if nothing else.

If *Mangus* is about transgressive bonding, *Whatever Happened to Julie Christie?* provides a comedic defense of civilized discourse. Conducted in a semi-vaudevillian register, *Julie Christie* is a discussion play. Entering semi-retirement, two friends—Jethro and Tyrone—engage in a quest to find out "if anybody knows anything." The actress Julie Christie presides over the search, an icon of hip sexiness. Like *Mangus*, the play hovers around the East Village. Jethro (Dr. Jethro Waldo, to be precise) is haunted by a memory of "a flotilla of fat women in wheelchairs selling dope." As if to keep the memory at bay, Jethro announces that he and Tyrone "have work to do." To find out more, Jethro launches a "survey" to "gather data" on "species devolution."

Once part of the counterculture, the two old men take inventory of the agenda of how things look forty years later. What happened and what didn't happen, who came out on top and what the young folk think about the whole deal. Echoes of Brecht's *Good Woman of Szechuan* can be heard, Murray deploying a gonzo version of Brecht's epic theater piece to explain Jethro's decidedly pataphysical mode of research:

"This is a study. Can't be too random. The idea is this: 'What is Man?' You use your best judgment, your best qualities. You attract the right people. You tape. You take careful notes, time and date, and so on, because the idea of memory comes in here."

The play diverges into a proliferation of exchanges with Jethro's beautiful scheming assistant Betsy. Various other semi-unhinged characters sign on to Jethro's pursuit of final clarity and understanding, the audience carried along on a rushing tide of lyrical thought, that singular music of the Mednick oeuvre. The play closes with the arrival of a Mexican kid in red shorts talking on the phone, a warning about the coming Trump dictatorship and also a reminder of our mortality. The most important thing is the tone—an adventurous irony along the familiar tropes of the quest narrative in a contemporary American world defined by shattered attention and reactivity.

This Judaic sub-genre within Murray's body of work—the discussion play—has a Talmudic dimension. *Three Tables* and *Two Violins* continue in this same vein. Both explore what might be called *ideational timing*—how the rhythms of thought line up in conversations between people and between groups of people separated by space and time. These plays showcase Murray's ear for the musicality of thought that is among his main gifts to theater lovers. A symbol of the Holocaust and of Judaica, the violin has a special significance to Murray. I recall the general astonishment in a workshop Murray held at his home in the late 1990s when he showed us the perfect violin he had crafted as a project in woodworking. A similar fineness can be heard in the nuanced, riffing poetry of these deeply felt plays—love songs to European Jewry by an American exile. In Three Tables, Murray uses repetition and monologues straight out to the audience to warn about the empty transactional reality to come.

The play *Death Sky Above* springs from another stream of Mednick's work—his engagement with Indigenous Americans. A white (Jewish) man named Painter hangs near the ceiling above the stage—a simulacrum of the painful ordeal embraced by some Amerindian tribes to bring visions.. Tending to him in his suffering is Leonard Crow Dog, a character based on the well-known Indigenous activist. Crow Dog befriended Murray during the creation of *The Coyote Cycle* (1978–86), and later invited him to sweats and other events on the Red Road. Together in *Death Sky Above*, the two men review a set of recurrent Mednick-ian concerns and tropes, eventually recruiting the audience to participate. The play invites adventurous theater artists to engage with some unique technical challenges, another regular feature of Murray's plays. Such challenges always deliver new understanding about the expressive potential of the stage and how it connects to the possibility of human meaning.

The final piece in this collection, *No Play,* follows the pursuit of a woman through a nightmarish world slipping back into primitive lawlessness. Unfolding in a mythical realm, *No Play* harkens back to Murray's full length *The Fool and the Red Queen*, part of *The Gary Plays* cycle we completed right before changes to the LA milieu—rising rents, the end of the 99-seat contract with Actor's Equity, and changes in state law that made freelance employment too costly—outran Padua's capacity to produce. *No Play* has the primal air of a blues ballad, lit up with calamity and woe. This strikes me as an entirely new note in Murray's extensive body of work. In his eighth decade this master craftsman continues to locate new paths to the waterfall.

The bespoke wonders of Mednick's work never fail to captivate—the way his dialogue stays true throughout to iambic meter, for example, providing performers with a magic carpet to ride into new worlds, the audience carried along for the ride. Also the compressed lyricism, the imagery so grounded in the body as to seem unadorned even while it shimmers with light from above. Also the vivid playfulness of his characters and the symphonic development of themes refracted through every gripping dramatic scene. It's the kind of hyper-developed style that in the fine arts often gets celebrated in retrospectives and other canonical events. Reduced by its role in providing passive entertainment, contemporary theater lags behind, leaving the task of discovering where true value lies to subsequent generations. This book is intended for those young artists—a thrilling bounty to discover and enjoy.

MANGUS THE MOTHERF*CKER

A PLAY BY MURRAY MEDNICK

Scene

A misty area, upstage darkened from whence the actors enter and exit. A large screen for projections. Optional.

Characters

Mangus	The Motherfucker.
Lark	His wife.
David	A lost soul.
Mr. Morris	A local resident.
Mr. and Mrs. Reed	Locals.
Roy Zinc	Another local.
A Policeman	Same as Roy Zinc.
A Jaguar Priest	
Voice Off	In italics, without parentheses.

The Universe is a scenario of non-simultaneous and only partially overlapping transforming events.

Mangus Here we are on the Event Horizon, where all falls and nothing is ever seen again.

Lark Where does it go?

Mangus No one knows.

Lark When do the skies clear?

Mangus I don't know.

Lark Great. What's taking so long?

Mangus It takes Time. Passing through worlds. Another world, another cosmos. Look. *(Projection)* Tidy streets and happy homes. The ideal America. 1947. I was eight years old. Never true, never the case. We were poor outcasts then and before then and before that and now, holding fast to our position. Keeping balance, some sort of equilibrium in the face of disaster, the end of worlds.

Mangus Bodies collapse into spiraling fragments, into nothing.

Lark We don't know, do we?

Mangus We do not. And yet I strive. Holding fast. An ideal. A way of life. A marriage.

Lark Electrons become spirals, which disappear. Nobody knows where it goes.

Mangus System's down. We need a map, a document, an image, a tone. A point. A closeup, a message, a portal, a pattern.

Lark Just stay off the booze, Mangus.

Mangus A Temple, a scroll. *(Ancient music.)* Ah.

Lark What's taking so long?

Mangus Progreso, Yucatán.

Lark Is what? A destination? A world?

Mangus A memory. Little Mayans coming to town with their bundles and wares. A walled compound. We were subsidized by the State. No, it was the Guggenheim Foundation. A livelihood guaranteed, upright, intact, except when I went on a spree, if I remember right, stealing vouchers in Campeche.

Lark Thought that was you.

Mangus Yes.

Lark Well, it's somewhat of a mystery. Off he went to the north, on a sailboat, I think it was.

Mangus Yes, it was. On a boat. A ferry.

Lark Was that you, Mangus?

Mangus It was.

Lark Say more.

Mangus Well, it was an affirmation in a way. Travelers' checks. American Express. Driving along the coast in my pick-up truck with my dog, Spot, smoking weed and drinking the Irish Whiskey that I got from Moyo. The whiskey and Lucky Strikes. Moyo ran that aspect of the town, sitting in the corner of the café rendering goods and services to the wandering gringos and their addictions.

Lark What was the affirmation?

Mangus I was affirming myself. That I could do something. Pull it off, you know. We had a group once. You were there. On the Lower East Side. We were Anarchists, we meant business. The Motherfuckers. Upending the System as much as we could. There was a War on.

Lark I think you blew up a storefront. I remember that. Between the park and the river.

Mangus Some gave their lives. Drugs and the cops. All dead now, though a few have disappeared, vanished into the mist.

Lark And the Yucatán?

Mangus We had an outpost there. We meant no harm. Remember Moyo? He was Arab. Lebanese. Kindly, but bigoted. A hard-ass. Sitting in the corner of the café like a dumpy god.

Lark Did he admire the angry gringos?

Mangus He acted as though he did.

Anything you want. All you must do is ask;
a week, ten days, it's yours.

Thanks a lot.

Mangus We paid court and gave him dollars. And he'd come through, you know, with a carton of Luckies, a bottle of Irish, cubes of hash. Good memories in the Yucatán.

Lark I got lost in the jungle around *Chichén-Itzá. (Photo)* Jaguars were there in those days.

Mangus Still are.

Lark I was terrified. Bad memories. Fuck that shit.

Mangus No angry talk now. Not now, Lark. We need to deal with the gravity of the situation. Not the time just now. Can't fuck with the Gravity.

Lark Don't lecture me.

Mangus It's like pedaling a bicycle on ice. Need to keep straight up and balanced and don't tip right or left. Can't slide or break your ride.

Lark Where are we now?

Mangus Hovering on the edge of black gravity itself. *(Sound)* Perhaps another dimension, in another body.

Repent, Motherfucker.

Mangus I'm sorry for everything I ever said or thought. Everything that I saw or heard or acted upon. All the lies and pretensions and faces and lies, the noise of falling or rising, grinding, pounding, stars colliding. Monsters in the mist, shining like spirits. The fog of war. Murder in the villages and towns. Murder in the household. Murder in the faces of love.

Murder in speech.

Mangus Fuck, man. The love obsessions, the lust obsessions, the gullibility. Married women. I regret that so much. Best friends' wives and all that. We couldn't see the consequences. Haunts me to this day. I'm so sorry.

Lark And you were drunk or stoned half the time.

Mangus No. I wasn't.

Lark Never mind.

Mangus Keep on keeping on and don't be afraid. And don't let up if you slip and fall, you get up again and trudge on, stay on course, or you're gone, lost in the event horizon.

Lark Another world.

Mangus Like was said, I don't think so.

Lark What, then?

Mangus Nothing then. *(Sound of sliding to a halt.)* Excuse me.

Lark Yes?

Mangus Did you take care of the car?

Lark I took care of the car.

Mangus Did you feed the kids?

Lark I fed the kids.

Mangus What did you feed them?

Lark Birds in their nests.

Mangus Very good.

Lark Melons and mice.

Mangus And the fighting?

Lark I stopped the fighting.

Mangus How so?

Lark I threw them into another time zone. They sang their death songs and vanished.

Mangus They will return.

Lark When?

Mangus I don't know when. Through a portal. They'll come back in through one of those.

Lark Only if we succeed.

Mangus Jaguars never fail. They go back into their lives like nothing ever happened. And no credit is ever given.

Lark Ah, as the story goes: we tried and tried and eventually we lost, crapped out, bowed down, paid our dues and skipped town. *(Pause)* I must ask—whose voice is this, singing of awful homicide? Of children thrown away like trash?

Mangus It's yours.

Lark And you?

Mangus Ah. Me. Well. The big cat prepares himself. He crawls back into his thoughts and wonders: a sperm and an egg, a spark of electricity, forming a mechanism that thinks, that remembers itself and knows what to do next.

Lark Memories: The Yucatán, the walled compound, the little Mayans arriving with their goods, their gifts, their solemnity. Progreso. Port silted up, a blue haze over the Gulf of Mexico.

Mangus Ancient sacrifice in the forest. Skulls fractured on the stones, blood on the stones. Frozen in time like endless wounds, ripe and red.

Lark If there's another world there, what would it be like?

Mangus Just like this one. *(Bangs his stick. The stage brightens.)*

Lark We could see the kids then, cavorting in the living room.

Mangus Did they go to school today on their bikes?

Lark *(Projection)* An interesting image, children on bikes, racing to school, laughing and shouting, and there on the hill waits the school, stony and sunny. Maple trees, perfect sidewalks, brand new cars, American cars, can't be beat.

Mangus Bums on the street, shit all over the place, lost hope, the evil eye. *A dollar, brother, gimme. Give me a dollar or I'll cut your throat.* He's brandishing a shiny machete. Where'd you get that fuckin' thing?

None of your fuckin' business white boy.

Mangus Lark?

Lark What?

Mangus Stand up.

Lark I'm standing, Motherfucker.

Mangus They have lunch at school?

Lark You bet they do.

Mangus That's good. Dangerous out there. Kids kidnapped for sex and money. Sex, money, and tortuous revenge.

Lark Where are we now?

Mangus Six miles to the west. Five fathoms down. High above the horizon, miles away from where we started. When we had an identity and a reason for living. No. We're in a foggy place in a different zone, where anything can happen.

Lark Everything has happened already.

Mangus Why do you say that?

Lark I've been here before. Exactly here. I feel the time passing. I feel like we're running out of time. I feel like everything has been done. I feel like everything is taking too long.

Mangus You contradict yourself.

Lark So, what?

Mangus We could go any which way now, but it's the violence holds us back for the moment.

Lark Violence?

Mangus From the locals.

Lark The locals? *(Sounds off)*

Mangus Yes, and we had best be alert.

Lark I am.

Mangus Come closer.

Lark Yes?

Mangus Did you walk the donkey today?

Lark I walked the donkey.

Mangus Did you perform fellatio today?

Lark Not today.

Mangus But you never do.

Lark You don't ask right.

Mangus It was all a ploy.

Lark I'm not a prostitute, I'm not a whore.

Mangus Nobody said so.

Lark Yeah, yeah.

Mangus And nobody thinks so.

Lark I feel faint now, as though the gravity has changed.

Mangus Hang on.

Lark I am hanging on.

Mangus What's my name?

Lark Mangus, the Motherfucker

Mangus What's my cause?

A trigger and a gun.

Lark And I?

Mangus You sing. Like an Angel. You have a sweet voice, and I could swallow you alive.

Lark Hold right there and don't fall.

Mangus Jaguars and birds of prey appear, birds with three wings and long beaks, beaks a foot long. *(Jungle sounds.)* Everything is electricity and nobody knows where it goes, spiraling into the void, or another cosmos, nobody knows.

Lark I was there. And in New York City. We had a canary that sang. *(Birdsong)*

Mangus *(Sounds of New York City)* The bank was around the corner. On the other corner was an elementary school. The park was up the street. My nephew was dying. Ned destroyed the apartment. It was alcohol that did it. We pulled the plug on the kid and then Ned the sonofabitch destroyed the apartment. *(Sounds of windows smashing.)*

Lark Ned?

Mangus His fuckin' name was Ned. Broke all the fuckin' windows. Who knows what to say about all this? I don't. Except I'd kill the sonofabitch if he wasn't dead already. We were anonymous, we had no glory. No one knew who we were. The Jaguars. Like ancient warriors pledged only to kill. The Eagles got the glory, while we got the job done. We struck swiftly and then we were gone, as though we were never there.

Lark And then?

Mangus We'd find a bar finally and sit down and get a drink finally and you'd say Ah, at last, so we could forget for a minute. The horror we couldn't quite digest, so it's a film now, a picture-show in the mind.

Lark *(Out, to Audience:)* Mangus the motherfucker, he ended up dead you know in a doorway. Nobody gave him a dime. He had no shirt on, his pants were greasy, and his mouth hung open, showing his rotten teeth. I saw him in a play one time, on the Bowery, and he had this monologue, which happened in the Yucatán. You were fucking someone else the whole time. It wasn't me at all, and yet you complained, like all assholes, you complained with your eyes, with your mouth, the way you stood in the hallway, that insolent posture.

Mangus Complained about what?

Lark About not getting laid. Nothing in your eyes but revenge. No love there. Silver and gold in your eyes—a thin line of silver there and gold shines like a dot where your pupils should be. You're not here. Like the Jaguar, you never are. Preoccupied. With memory and thoughts, and images appearing and murderers to find. In my own life as well.

Mangus We must remain as neutral, Lark, as we can. Tell me: How does love end?

Lark Does it ever end? I don't think so. Even a shadow, even a hint.

Mangus Maybe not.

Lark No.

Mangus Maybe it exists in time. Just a matter of time.

Lark It's taking too long.

Mangus Be patient.

Lark I am.

Mangus Sing a song.

Lark No. I'll tell you my dream. If you'll pay attention, motherfucker.

Mangus Okay, go.

Lark First: By what Law does the Jaguar play?

Mangus The Law of murder. Silent and invisible.

Lark And what is his prey?

Mangus Run and hide, those who run and hide.

Lark Good. So. And in walks a killer—he's got a Jaguar mask and body armor and a machine gun—he barricades himself into a classroom—holy shit he thinks, I can do whatever I feel like doing while the dumb police wait outside.

Mangus Texas. The cornball state, where everybody is Americanized. Guns in the street, moronic fantasies.

Lark So, the cops stand outside while the lunatic opens fire and kills nineteen ten-year-olds and two teachers. All immigrants from Mexico with Mexican names. Why were you guys standing around outside?

Well, we didn't know.

We thought it was over.

We thought it was on the other side, in another building.

Lark You stupid fuck, you're dumb and terrified. You're looking right at it.

We didn't know.

Lark You're dumb and Americanized, lost in Cowboy films, where the bystanders don't intervene while the shootout happens in the street and the Mexicans and Indians fall wildly off their horses.

Mangus Right!

Lark You dumb fucks. I hope you die a thousand deaths. *(Pause)* The police were hanging around wondering what to do. I hope they go on trial and hang. I hope they die.

Mangus You hope everybody dies, Lark.

Lark Everybody does die.

Mangus Okay, go on, Lark.

Lark Well, I walked in there and opened fire. They were all dead already, I just put a big red spot on their chests. I'm done, now. I'm done. We're somewhere else now, in another world. It's called:

DREAMS OF AN ANCIENT TRIBE

Lark I don't know what that means.

Mangus I don't either.

Lark You go first.

Mangus Did you blame the conquistadors today?

Lark May they be eaten by their horses.

Mangus It's nightmares, mainly, Lark.

Lark Is what?

Mangus Waking up sullen. Vague, disappointing imagery, slightly wet in your pants. And still the day is ahead of you.

Lark Not much of a day. A long night, maybe. Got to cleanup. Tend to the children. I want to weep, for the way it is, the way things are, and I will, like the murderess goddess of the night in Teotihuacan—shed her tears of blood.

Mangus *(Out)* The boy feels hurt, abused. He goes into the dense forest feeling sorry for himself, angry. This powerful inner turmoil becomes his friend. He doesn't
let go of it for a long time. Later, when they turn on him, he goes into himself for his friend. Their habitation is a grinding death machine from which there is no escape, a forestry of implacable temptation. But thoughts of copulation are now tinged with repugnance. A sense of swinish helplessness—he has become the victim of unspeakable husbandry, a farm animal.

Lark *(Out)* All faces are now false faces, masking a secret suffering, a blind, useless sorrow, a violent disgust. The faces talk. They can't stop talking.

I didn't do it.

I didn't mean to do it.

I'll never do it again.

Mangus There's no time to breathe. The ashtrays fill with blackening blood. He hangs his head in shame.

Lark Suddenly she catches herself in a lie. It's a machination from childhood, a familiar pose. There's arrogance in it, and ferocity. She hears it in her voice. It's all out there on the table, like a writhing lizard with bright red eyes and a forked tongue. It will follow her through the long night ahead.

Lark Hi! The frightened boy says.

Mangus Hello!

Name's Ned.

Lark No! Ned fell into the Gowanus Canal—bad fentanyl, a hot shot did him in. Shit came all the way from Mexico.

Name's Moyo!

Mangus I don't think so. Hammer and nail. Banged through his head by a Persian spy. God knows why.

Oh!

Mangus My name is Mangus. Pay attention.

Okay!

Mangus It's a dream. We were driving. We drove on a highway to the top of the world, up into the sky. How could such a road have ever been built? On we climbed. The ascent became vertical, straight up. I gasped for breath. I thought, "This car doesn't have the power for this, this car will fall off the road." We hung in the balance, on the edge of falling. "Why have they put this highway here, this must be some kind of test." "No, this is a tourist road, this is for sightseers." Was it a mountain, or a city made of rock? We were heading for the highest point of all the cities of all the worlds.

Thank you.

Lark I'll do one now. It's called The American Town. You want to imagine—the yellow lighting, weeds along the railroad tracks, red brick walls, the store windows, the drunk on Main Street, parking meters. A waning afternoon on the edge of town. A shiny car goes by. We know the nickname of the driver. He cruises in his Oldsmobile slowly through his town and down the road. It's as though his eyes are in his chest or on the fenders of his car. The radius of his vision includes the road, the telephone poles, the last houses right and left. Boundaries from his boyhood. He is keeping something hidden which is known by everyone in town. He takes it with him down the road and into the woods.

Applause.

Mangus He is a Seeker the likes of whom has never been seen in all the worlds, the stars above and the stars below.

Lark Where is this guy?

Mangus He cannot be seen with ordinary eyes.

Oh!

Mangus Woman next door. She's attractive. Husband's a fathead. Likes cherry bombs and talks loud on the phone.

Lark Keep your pants on.

Mangus It's electricity, it's all in the electromagnetism of everything. Desire.

Lark Yeah, yeah.

Mangus Otherwise, it's—you can't explain it. Lovely woman. Two kids.

Lark Leave it alone.

Mangus Where are the children now?

Lark Swimming.

Mangus There's water in the pool?

Lark Of course, there's water in the pool. Uh-oh.

Hey, you know anything about Bellevue?

Lark No.

You know if they tell you about O.D.'s?

Lark No.

They gave me some pills and they told me to take one a day, two at the most. I took thirteen of 'em.

Lark When?

Yesterday. I don't know what happened. And that doesn't happen to me, where I don't know what happened. Someone saved my life and I'd like to thank the guy.

Lark What's your name?

David.

Lark Hi.

Hi.

Lark Where do you live? *(Enter David)*

David Down aways a few miles down the foggy coast you got to watch out or you'll drown yourself in the dark-dark sea.

Lark Oh.

Mangus How do you live?

David We farm the sea. We use artificial light on the seabed. We grow a variety of kelp and a certain vine. Not radioactive.

Lark I shouldn't think so.

David We feed the dead sun with garbage. And they fire asteroids and little frozen hydrogen bullets into it.

Lark Why?

David I don't know why. Maybe to wake it up. And you?

Lark What?

David Shoot bullets?

Lark Yes, all over the place. It's like the Wild West. Everybody is armed.

David Wow.

Lark *(Projection)* This is a view of our galaxy, the Milky Way. Far away. Very far away. And this is a shot of an ancient Aztec calendar. A sun-face in the center. The Aztecs could measure enormous lengths of time. *(Image of an Aztec priest in his black regalia, hair matted with blood, plunging a stone knife into a sacrificial victim, then pulls out the pulsing heart.)* They did this to keep the Sun moving across the sky.

David Across the sky!

Lark Yes.

Mangus It is said that the gods gathered in the twilight of Teotihuacan. And one of them, a leprous god covered in boils, threw himself into a huge brazier as a sacrifice. He rose from the blazing coals changed into a Sun. But he was motionless. He needed blood in order to move. So, the gods immolated themselves and the Sun, drawing life from their deaths, began its course across the sky. This was the beginning of a cosmic drama in which humanity took on the role of the gods, to keep the Sun moving in its course so that darkness should not rule the world forever, it was necessary to feed it every day with its food, the "precious water"—human blood.

David Human blood!

Lark Yes. *(As David gags and writhes.)* I don't know why I showed him that material, Mangus.

Mangus What came up on the screen, what it was.

David What it was.

Mangus Yes.

Lark Pull yourself together.

David Oh. Pull myself together. Yes. Nice stick you have there.

Mangus Yeah.

David Is that a Jaguar on there?

Mangus That's a jaguar.

David That's a Jaguar. Oh.

Mangus I've always had this stick.

David Oh. I think I must go home now.

Mangus Thanks for coming by.

David Thanks for coming by.

Mangus You're welcome.

David I'll come again if I can, if you don't mind, if it's alright, thank you very much.

Lark You're welcome anytime.

David You're welcome. Anytime. Thank you.

Mangus Okay, bye-bye.

David Bye.

Mangus Bye, now. *(David exits.)* Weird.

Lark He repeats himself.

Mangus He repeats us. The last thing said.

Lark How odd.

Mangus He reminds me of something. A guy. A war veteran. American. Marine. Like Ned. He comes home and throws his wife down the stairs and beats her to death. But it wasn't him that did it. It was another him that did it, and they're not in touch. Same person. One guy likes men and the other one's a family man. And one of 'em is the killer. Guess which one did it.

Lark I can't tell.

Mangus Right. And neither can he. And he's so good at being the good guy, he gets away with it for the most part, because all he must do is act the good guy who is right and true and no one's the wiser.

Lark How do you know?

Mangus Nice American town. Nice looking kids. Green rolling hills of the Appalachians. The American Way. Can't say no more, the moral rightness of a thing. He's on my list, the sonofabitch.

Lark Take a breath. Look out, Mangus. Look. I can't get over how it looks outside. You can't see so well in the fog, but you get down by the ocean and you see the rocks they have here shining up at you from the beach. They glisten like stars. Standing there at the point, you have the impression that the sky is all around you, above and below.

Mangus Could be the amount of carbon in the water, as in coal. I mean, is why the ocean is so black.

Lark Why the ocean is so black. Yes. I think that's right.

Mangus Had it in the old days, mark of the Motherfuckers, gang of outcasts, we had tattoos and amulets and a scarf and a belt, and so on. Insignia. Sign of the Jaguar. It's a gift. When we were hunting down the Nazi killers in South America.

Lark Okay, don't point it at me.

Mangus We killed without mercy.

Lark I know you did.

Mangus Why so moody?

Lark I don't understand what's taking so long.

Mangus Conditions must be just right. All the gravitational and tidal effects must be blocked. We can go out there and never come back. The tide is faster than the fastest tide on Earth. The fog is the worst I've ever seen.

Lark What's that coming at us? *(Enter Mr. and Mrs. Reed)*

Mr. Reed Don't be afraid, ma'am. It's only us.

Mrs. Reed We won't hurt you.

Mr. Reed Difficult typography, right here.

Mrs. Reed We've adapted well, I think.

Mr. Reed We're the Reeds. The Reeds have maintained the lighthouse for generations.

Mrs. Reed Did our son come by here? He gets lost at times. Fog too much for him.

Mr. Reed Life's too much for him.

Mrs. Reed Never mind.

Mangus Yes, he was by here. Then he left.

Mr. Reed Long night.

Lark Yes, it is.

Mr. Reed Suggestibility is what it is.

Lark And he repeats.

Mr. Reed Tell him to come on home.

Mangus We will, sir. Ma'am.

Mrs. Reed Thank you.

Mr. Reed Name's David.

Mangus Right.

Mr. Reed Bye, bye.

Lark Bye. *(Foghorn. Enter David)*

Mangus Holy shit, here he is now, appearing out of the fog.

David Good evening.

Mangus Go on home kid, your parents are looking for you.

David Looking for me.

Mangus Yes.

David Fog is dense this evening.

Mangus Yes, it is.

David Yes, it is. The black sun is like a seed.

Mangus No, it isn't.

David The whole universe collapses into it.

Lark He has a point there.

David Souls out there getting ready in the dark.

Mangus For what?

David For what?

Mangus That's what I asked you.

David It is said that they are the souls of the dead who are not at peace with themselves and so they come out to argue. They come out searching for people to talk to so they can explain how their lives went wrong and argue as to how it should have gone differently with them.

Lark Do they know who you are?

David Who?

Lark Them.

David I don't know.

Lark That would be important, wouldn't it?

David Important. I don't know.

Lark You don't know squat.

David A ghost is someone who doesn't want to die. His head is still going. Like a slot machine. He doesn't know what's happening, so he hangs around.

Lark What's taking so long?

David What's—

Lark Don't repeat me.

Mangus You are here because you are lost, and you want to take a short cut home.

Lark Something like that.

David And you?

Lark What?

David You're afraid of getting old and dying in space.

Lark So true.

David So true.

Mangus Best to get back to your mom and dad.

David I should learn to play an instrument. Pass the time. I like your walking stick.

Mangus Thank you.

David Hand-carved Jaguar. I was wondering, do you have a text?

Mangus A text?

David A book or a scroll.

Lark No.

David No, perhaps a map, a celestial map. A map of the skies?

Mangus I might have one.

Lark Lots of maps.

David I'll come back.

Lark No!

David Well, I seem to have over-stayed my presence.

Lark So long.

David Oh. One more thing. *(Enter Mr. Morris)* This is Mr. Morris. He wanted to meet you.

Lark How do you do?

Mr. Morris Very well, thank you.

Lark Bye-bye for now, David.

Mangus Good night, David.

David Bye now. *(Exits)*

Mr. Morris I think if people would leave each other alone, life would be a lot easier. When I was young, I wanted to know things. Now I just leave it alone.

Lark Good idea.

Mr. Morris I thought I was going places. Making progress. Scratching around. I'm settled down now, I leave it alone. I go out on the beaches occasionally, collect my rocks, do my job.

Lark What is your job?

Mr. Morris I run the lighthouse. I keep an eye on things. I don't bother anybody.

Lark Good for you.

Mr. Morris Yes, it is. You said that. Very good. Generations of being here. Quiet. Fastest tide in the world. And they say it's getting warmer, a degree or two per generation. Probably why you're keen to investigate.

Mangus Yes, it is.

Mr. Morris Well, you take the tides now—they're tricky, the tides are. A man could be down to Refugee Cove, down there off the point, and get caught by the tide. He wouldn't be able to get back. It's a problem we have here with the moon. A man got lost on the moor, year or two ago, found him on the rocks. He'd fallen down the sheer side of a cliff there in a storm and broke his neck.

Mangus The moon?

Mr. Morris Unpredictable. Of course, wasn't always as peaceful. Couple hundred years ago they chased the Russians out, cornered 'em down in the cove, that's how they call it Refugee Cove. Most of 'em died. You can still see the graves, anchored to cables a mile or so out to sea.

Lark Mangus?

Mangus What?

Lark The Russians?

Mangus The Russians.

Lark Say good-bye to Mr. Morris.

Mr. Morris I'm a rock-picker. I pick rocks. Small rocks. Any kind of small rock. They shine like little stars. I use them for my fireplaces. I glue them on for ornament. It's very nice. They're only about twelve inches high and ten across. Pieces of red glass inside. I put some carbon product on the red glass and plug a light into it and she glows. I sold five of them last week. Woman up to the station at Apple River. She gave one each to some sisters of hers, I believe. A couple more she used for wedding presents. They make a nice gift.

Mangus I'll bet they do.

Lark Very nice.

Mr. Morris I'm here for three weeks now. Been here two weeks already. Then I go up to Cape Enrage until the 36th... That'll be two weeks off around New Year ten thousand long nights ago. You can have this rock here. It's a power rock.

Mangus A power rock?

Lark Where did it come from?

Mr. Morris Fell out of the sky, as you'd expect. Power came with it. See, I'm taking the assistant's place five weeks altogether. Makes four weeks' vacation plus another week owed to him. That's down to the lighthouse here. You been down there to see the beacon? Inter-galactic beacon, you know. Ain't too many of those. Aimed at Andromeda, that way. *(Points)* Won't get there for a million years. Government wants to let them know we're out here. Mainly it's to orientate the ships coming in. Come down with me some night and I'll show you the beacon.

Mangus You bet. Cosmic power falling.

Lark Word dust falling.

Mr. Morris They put a freeze on 'em last year. A freeze came up out of the Government put a stop to vacations. Don't know why that happened. This year has been a good year though. See, the boss has got to take his vacation soon as Roy comes back. That's Roy Zinc lives over at Station Three, West Monitor, one that watches where the Sun used to be.

Mangus Well—

Mr. Morris He's gone up to Squally Point for a week and then he's not sure, but he's got another two weeks. Sick leave is not the same as vacation, you see.

Lark 'Course not—

Mr. Morris Someone gets sick, or something happens, they call on me. Before I took Roy's place, I was over to Chinecto Station taking my cousin's place, that's Philip Morris, my name's Chester.

Mangus Interesting.

Mr. Morris I was filling in for him three weeks. They've got a light down there, but no horn. Ought to have a horn. I don't care how narrow the gap is, the fog is tricky. You might know it.

Mangus Sure do.

Mr. Morris But I'm not the man quarrels with the authorities. If there's two ways to do a thing, the boss's way and the right way, it's the boss's way I'll want to do it. Now, the boss here—he's Mr. Murphy, his people are down in Parsbury—anyway, he won't take a drink himself, so he forbids it. But me and Reg Fleming—he's the third man on here—me and him will drink a quart of an evening and no one is the wiser. What he doesn't know won't bother him is what we say. So long as it's not interfering with our duties. I'm a man that's reliable. I'm on time and I'm steady. My brother is an alcoholic. *(To Mangus)* You're not one, are you?

Mangus No. I don't think so.

Mr. Morris I've got a fireplace down to the lighthouse that I'll show you. Another coat of varnish and it's done. I'll do that tonight. Sold to a woman at East Prosecute Station. She has one already. I sell 'em for twelve dollars. *(Pause)* Costs two to make one. I've got another one just ready for the rocks. Have it done by tomorrow.

Lark No, thanks.

Mangus We have other business.

Mr. Morris Like what?

Lark Find our way home and such.

Mangus Work to do, things to see and organize.

Mr. Morris I work steady. Right on through. Then I put a coat of varnish on 'em and drill a hole for the electric wire. Due the twenty-third. Lady up at Advocate Station, lives with her two sisters on Main Street. You ever hunt moose?

Mangus What?

Mr. Morris I'll tell you a moose yarn. My friend Rudy Dewis and me—oh, I known Rudy almost my whole life—Rudy's a cripple, you know, he was born with his feet turned around the wrong way. They tried to break his feet to make them right. Didn't work. Made 'em worse. But he *loves* to hunt moose. He's very interested in hunting and fishing. Things like that, even with his twisted feet. And we were walking along one morning, and I had my old twelve with me and Rudy had his brand new thirty-odd-six. And he was fired up he'd see a moose. He'd just got his moose license, and he was hopeful of getting a shot at one. He was holding onto my arm, naturally, because of his crippled feet. Whadyaknow but up comes this moose a hundred yards away from us. Well, Rudy couldn't get his rifle aimed in time, so I raised up and shot him with my old twelve-gauge, using my free arm of course, and I got him. I gave him to Rudy though. Didn't mean much to me and I knew it meant a lot to him. We went down to his hunting shack and had a feast. You ever ate any moose?

Mangus No.

Lark I don't think so.

Mr. Morris Tastes better than a cow, if you ask me. My cousin, Philip Morris, he's got one arm. He got sick. Weighs two hundred pounds, but he got sick. His house is smaller than mine and he has *four* children. *(Ominous silence)* I've lived alone, myself, these long, long nights. You'll want to keep an eye out for that Reed boy.

Lark David?

Mr. Morris Could be anywhere now. Killed his parents, ya know. Cut their hearts out of 'em. Did it to 'em live. Hearts are gone. Took 'em with him, I reckon. Don't know why he did that. Found the weapon. Stone knife, made of these same rocks, found it shining in shallow water off the point. Oh, you'll want to keep to the vicinity and hold your ship aground for a while.

Lark Are there other boys?

Mr. Morris Of course. Yes. They have little black spots all over them. Running around. Having a good time.

Lark Black spots? *(Projection)*

Mr. Morris Yes, like a Jaguar. Or a monkey. You take pills?

Mangus Yes.

Mr. Morris Why?

Mangus To avoid pain. To avoid fear.

Lark Go on.

Mangus To avoid oppression. To avoid consequences.

Lark That's not all.

Mangus To avoid injustice. To avoid emotion. To avoid defeat. To have something to look forward to. To have an excuse. To avoid the stench. To avoid lying. To avoid boredom.

Lark Enough, already.

Mangus To avoid lying.

Mr. Morris Well, good luck with that. You have kids?

Lark Two boys.

Mr. Morris Lock 'em up. Lock 'em up and throw away the key.

Lark Why do such a thing?

Mr. Morris Machine-gunner walks in and kills 'em all. Bang-bang! *(Sounds of gunfire.)* All gone! A bloody mess! Here's a communique:

The body of Mrs. Roy Zinc of West Monitor Station has been discovered off Squally Point at 0800. Her heart was torn from her chest with a blunt instrument. They suspect that the killer, David Reed, is still at large.

Mr. Morris So, I'd keep an eye out if I were you. Thanks. *(Exits)*

Mangus Take a hike.

Lark Bye, bye.

Mangus Get lost. Where are the kids, Lark?

Lark I let them out to play.

Mangus You let them out to play?

Lark I let them out to play. *(Pause)*

Mangus Where are they now?

Lark How the fuck should I know?

Mangus You don't know?

Lark No. They must be at school, playing ball in the schoolyard.

Mangus Where were you?

Lark I was asleep, I think. Taking a nap. *(Sounds)* I could hear the ball outside, skipping around, and children playing. *(Sounds of a marital argument)* Uh-oh.

Mangus What is it?

HELP!

Take your hands off me!

She's trying to kill me!

I'm taking the kids!

Like hell you are!

Call the police!

Lark They're fighting next door. He's such a jerk, playing the victim. So typical.

Mangus She's very cool.

Lark I know she is. Keep your head straight. *(Pause)* I had a dream. You listening, Motherfucker? I was looking for my shoes. I came to a house where some friends were having a party. They offered me a drink and I sat down. I waited for a while, but no one returned. They had all gone away. I left the house and walked through a courtyard. I was looking for my shoes. The sky was splendid with wonderful colors, but something warned me not to look up.

Don't look up.

Lark That if I were to look up into the sky, I would lose all chance of ever finding my shoes. In the courtyard, I met a man with oily black hair. He was holding a pair of shoes. He gave them to me but when I tried to put them on, they didn't fit. They weren't mine. I became frightened and ran away from the man. Then there was another man, a funny little guy holding another pair of shoes. He was smiling. He seemed to know me. I tried on the shoes, and they didn't fit. The little man suffered.

The Little Man.

Lark He said I should go on to the next house.

Go on to the next house.

Lark There were some people there who would help me. I said I must really find my shoes. He said that he understood that everything would be alright.

Everything will be alright.

Lark He was sad. *(Music. Video.)* I began to feel drawn to the music coming from the other house. I went up the stairs into that house. People greeted me without paying any attention to me, but they were not unfriendly. A woman came close. I told her that I was looking for my shoes and that my friends in the other house had offered me a drink and then gone away, which made me feel bad. She was middle-aged and had brown curly hair and she was in pain. She said that although she had just arrived, she was sure that I would be able to find my shoes. She herself had lost her heart and would never find it again. I tried to say something kind. She waved me away, saying: "We would be glad to offer you a drink, but there's nothing to mix it with." I started to answer that I'd be happy to take it straight, but she was no longer listening. I realized there was a party going on. The music was coming from upstairs. The party was on the roof! As I climbed toward the roof, I saw the comet! It filled half the sky and was made of all the colors of the rainbow streaming across the black sky! LOOK! LOOK UP!

Look up! (Projection—Comet)

Lark LOOK AT THE COMET! LOOK! LOOK! I wanted to leap into the sky and become a part of that beautiful comet forever, but my body—

Mangus It's gone now.

Lark It's gone. I think she was a very nice lady.

Mangus Yeah.

Lark In my dream.

Mangus Right.

Lark And you?

Mangus Did you appease the Mullah today?

Lark What kind of question is that? You're out of your fuckin' mind!

Mangus Sorry.

Lark Where were you, Motherfucker?

Mangus I had been walking for a long time, in Mexico, the Yucatán, angry that there had been nowhere to go, no one to visit, when I came to a café—a pale, blue light in a darkened street. I was thirsty and went directly to the counter, where there was a lady wearing a red dress and red shoes. Bright red. And she wore red-jeweled earrings. And her lips were painted red and there was red shadow around her narrow blue eyes. She looked at me with disdain, shaking her head, her shiny black hair almost striking me. I made the gesture of one drinking from a bottle. She nodded, handed me a cold, black beer, and smiled. I felt embarrassed by my anger and smiled profusely. She mumbled something, shrugged, and walked away. She knew how my eyes were on her hips as she walked, a gaze like hardened electric light. A wire.

Lark And then?

Mangus Look. *(Video)* I sat down at a table near the door. Everything was blue—table, chairs, floors, walls, ceiling—all blue. The café faced onto a square. Directly across the way was a great old stone church framed in orange electric light. A windowless red bus was parked on the corner.

Shrouded forms were climbing on and off the bus in a desperate hurry. As I watched the bus, trying to understand what was going on, I became aware of the drone of conversation in the café . They were speaking an ancient musical language I had never heard before. Then I became frightened. The language these people were speaking was an extinct Mayan tongue, *Lacondon*. I don't know how I knew this with such certainty.

Pause.

Mangus I looked up and caught the woman in the red dress watching me as though she knew my thoughts. For a moment, I was overwhelmed by a tremendous sexual longing for her. She was aware of this and smiled sardonically as she moved from table to table, her wide hips swaying in the tight red dress.

Pause.

Mangus At the table nearest me, three young men were whispering intensely. I was sure that they were discussing my presence there and that if they knew my thoughts and desires, they would attack me. I indignantly stared at the red floor, trying to concentrate. Suddenly two beggars appeared, a woman and a child, their outstretched hands covered with sores. I started to give them money, but the woman refused and spat on the money. Then I noticed two groups of people passing back and forth in front of the café. Two young girls flanked a crippled old lady. The old lady had to swing one leg in a 180-degree arc in order to walk.

Somehow, I understood that the girls were talking about the consciousness of spiders and worms, while the old woman giggled continually. The other group was composed of three young Indian men. The one in the middle would turn towards me and make a face. He would show his teeth in a wide mask-like grin, flaring his nostrils and rolling his eyes. His teeth were jagged, filed down to a point in the ancient way. Each time they passed I became more deeply enraged by that face. Again and again, they passed, and that grotesque Indian showed that horrible mask. Finally, I hurled myself out into the street and went for him. I wanted to cut into that face with my broken beer bottle—we rolled together on the pavement. I was stabbing at his face—it was the face of a Jaguar—

(A red-light flash on and off.)

Killer on the loose. Wants the Sun to rise and thrive. His latest victims were Mr. and Mrs. Avril Hope, sea-bed farmers from East Prosecute Station. Time of the murders is believed to be 0955. The Governor General has called for a state of emergency—

Lark What do we do?

Mangus I don't know. Call the cops?

Lark And then what? Everything is taking so long. I don't understand it. *(Light cue.)*

Mangus It's twilight.

Lark Interesting: Radioactive light.

Mangus My fondest time of day or night.

Lark Mine as well. I love the light. Listen. Listen up.

Mangus I'm listening.

Lark I dreamt that I had become you, Mangus, that I was inside of you. I was inside you, but I was also myself. I could feel what you were thinking and feeling, but I was outside also, like a spirit. I remember thinking: "I don't want to be here; this isn't where I was meant to be. I hope this will be over soon."

Mangus I love you, Lark. I don't understand why. It's an unmistakable, overwhelming feeling, that look we exchanged, the gaze, only a moment, complete, unalterable, final, flashing like a goddess or a lightning bolt.

Lark Not the lightning bolt.

Mangus No.

Lark And then comes the daily grind, the kids, the job, the shit and piss and worry of it all.

Mangus Yes.

Lark Let me finish.

Mangus Please.

Lark It was a world in another solar system, and you were a soldier. We were marching, marching. I could sense your fatigue and your longing. I could feel your breath, the scent of alcohol, tequila, I could feel your breathing. The terrain was a wasteland, with ditches and trenches and weird canyons everywhere. We were marching along, knowing we were all going to be destroyed. The people around us, the other soldiers, an officer, I couldn't trust them. They might do anything, stupidly, insanely, and get us killed. I kept trying to talk to you, to ask you to take me away from that place. And I knew you heard me because I was speaking with *your* mind. But we couldn't MOVE. We could DECIDE, but we could not MOVE. And then we came to an area that had just been bombed. There were stacks of bodies in neat rows. I mean, piles of mangled flesh. And through each pile there were stuck FOUR bombs. I don't know why FOUR, but four bombs like huge fat arrows. And the stacks of bodies went on and on into the distance. On and on. The most terrible thing was the stench. It was so vivid. A voice, it was an officer, was saying, "Well, this is what happens when you get bombed. These are the bombs. They come from the enemy." A soldier reached into a pile and pulled off an arm, and then—a heart! I was shouting Mangus! Mangus! With your own voice. I was so desperate I began to come back, to wake up. I was coming away from the smell of death, and I was only free of it when I could no longer, no longer actually smell the piles of dead meat and burnt alcohol and with those four bombs sticking through them like arrows.

Mangus Well. *(Pause)* The only thing really, the only thing given us, is a taste of Paradise.

Lark Oh, come on.

Mangus I'd like to track the woman next door, press her against the wall and kiss her hard, and then lift her dress—

A loud knock at the door.

David (Off): Let me in! Let me in!

Mangus It's David. *(David appears, covered in blood.)*

Mangus What do you want?

David A map! Document!

Lark Go away!

Mangus We have nothing! We've lost our way! We're waiting!

David For what?

Mangus For the skies to clear!

David For the skies to clear! You must be fucking kidding! You must be fucking kidding!

Lark Get moving!

David I'll be back!

Lark Don't come back!

David I'll be back! *(Exits)*

Lark I hope he dies out there. He's leaving little pieces of death all over us, like lice.

Mangus Get away! Get them off! Get them away from me! *(Drumbeat as he writhes.)*

Lark Calm down. He's gone.

(A silence. Mr. Zinc appears. He is a Peter Lorre type plastic-skinned native. He carries a large axe over his shoulder.)

Lark Who's that? Who's there?

Zinc Zinc's the name. Roy Zinc.

Lark What do you want?

Zinc Having a bit of trouble?

Mangus What do you mean?

Zinc Saw you flopping on the ground. Thought it might be the murdering Reed kid. Killed his parents, you know.

Lark We do know.

Zinc Shot 'em in the face. Tore their hearts out. This fella here has a bad voice.

Mangus Sore throat.

Zinc That a fact?

Mangus That's a fact.

Zinc No need to be ill-tempered.

Lark There you go.

Mangus Shut up, Lark.

Zinc I catch him I'm going to kill him outright. But first I'll torture him, I'll suck up his power. I'll take the last quantum of juice from his soul. Then I'll hang him. He'll float on the dark sea for eternity, locked to a steel cable. Twenty-two fathoms down off Cape Enrage. During the long nights I'll row out to his grave and spit into his memory.

Mangus Right up your alley, Lark.

Lark Thanks a lot and fuck you.

Zinc Ought to leave him to us. Keep to your own business. She liked shoes. Mrs. Zinc. It was shoes she liked best. She liked to work with them, give them care. A woman's different, she's got special needs. Takes years, learn a woman's heart. Deep and dusky. Liked shoes. You make a pattern, fills the long nights.

Mangus What's your name again, sir?

Zinc Zinc. Roy Zinc. Listen close to my meaning: the killer is one of us. You don't belong out here. We don't want you. Stumbling around, giving warning. We'll hunt him down. He'll be coming back here, back to his starting point.

Lark Here?

Zinc *(Whirling his axe, making a rainbow of light.)* Walking about in the fog, might get one of these, slash your skull, mash your brains. Be misfortunate. *(Pause)* She liked shoes. Shoes and the music of the organ. *(Exits. Music.)*

Lark Nasty old gink.

Mangus Where are the boys?

Lark They went out to play, like I told you.

Mangus Did you pay the nanny?

Lark I paid the nanny.

Mangus Did you pay the dealer?

Lark I paid the dealer.

Mangus Look.

Lark I'm looking.

Mangus My father used to sit like this, just this way. I catch myself doing something and it isn't me at all, it's him. Poor old fuck fell off a building and cracked his skull. Never recovered. Thought the truth of a thing lay in the force of its presentation. He acted as though his life were on the line all the time, as if his life was his own creation.

Lark Maybe he was right. I taught school for many years, as you know. It develops, I don't know what to call it, a kind of heavy empathy. A sense of Fate, maybe, of consequence.

Mangus The last time I saw him on Planet Earth he was living in Mexico, where he could maintain his habits on his army pension. We hadn't been in contact for years. I didn't want to start anything up with him, just wanted to look at him. He was easy to find, the only gringo gimp in town, living in the one hotel on the square. I sat on a bench and waited while a little humped-back kid shined my shoes. This kid had the harsh, sour voice of an old man. He made me think of Caliban and old trolls. Finally, my father showed up, hobbling on the arm of a kindly-looking, bent-over Indian woman. He stared at the pavement, noticing nothing. He seemed almost blind. His face was grey and decrepit. I knew that he was going to die soon, and he knew it as well, that in fact he was nearly dead. The only thing alive about him were the movements of his fingers as he clutched the woman's shoulder. I think he loved her.

Lark Did you stay?

Mangus No. He didn't recognize me. I went back, I missed the street, the greasy, hazy, crackling, hard-concrete, give-no-quarter New York streets. *(N.Y. Sounds. Projection.)* You could get lost, you know, downtown, empty streets, you don't know what the fuck happened or how the hell you got there. *(Sound of police siren.)* Uh-oh. It's the cops.

Lark What the fuck. *(Enter Policeman)*

Policeman Well, well, a monkey-man.

Mangus Fuck off.

Policeman God forbid someone should say something bad about you.

Lark Are you blind, are you deaf and blind? Like the fearful cops of yore?

Mangus *(To Policeman)* Are you calling me a monkey?

Policeman May I sit?

Mangus Sit.

Policeman Wrong side of the Universe. Bouncing about, adventuring, falling here and there. I'm here to tell you—

Lark So, what?

Policeman This world is an electrical system in which everything is connected through an electromagnetic forcefield by a superluminal process that makes the knowledge of all events simultaneous and instantaneous.

Mangus What does that fucking mean?

Policeman Quarantine on the planet. Nothing comes in, nothing goes out. Messy business set in motion here. Psychopathological.

Mangus Meaning?

Policeman Meaning, we know where the kid is.

Lark Where's that?

Policeman Close by.

Lark You're just a bunch of chickenshit cowboys in funny hats all gunned up and quivering in your boots.

Mangus Ease up, Lark.

Lark No.

Policeman You are the crime. It's you.

Mangus How so?

Policeman By showing that kid Mexican sacrificial murder, cutting out folks' hearts so the Sun— There's an electronic wind—

Mangus That what?

Policeman Causes dreams and memories to erupt. And warps Time and Space. But you will pay. Time comes 'round and payment's due. And that's how it goes.

Lark Oh. Where are my boys?

Policeman What kind of mother are you?

Lark The best kind. You fuck and get the result. Plugged in.

Out comes the boys. And you feed 'em and watch 'em because they give back Love, a connection to Reality, and somehow, they got a role to play in the Future, in Time, but it's pain and suffering all the way home. Excuse me. You got that?

Policeman Here they are.

(Amplified) Hi, Mom!

Lark Thank you.

Mangus A colossal misunderstanding.

Policeman I'll be going now. I'll be on my way.

Lark Bye, bye.

Policeman Don't be such a bitch. Won't get you squat. But who gives a shit? No avoiding you get what you deserve. It's a Law. Right up your dreamy ass. I'm a butt man myself, never got over it. I look and look and keep on looking. 'Course, they don't look back, don't even see me at all, seems like. *Adios, y bien futura. (Exits)*

(Sound of foghorn)

Mangus Listen. *(Out, to Audience)* It was a dark, overcast night, no stars, no moon. The electric lights, weak because of insufficient power, gave everything a gaudy, yellowish tint. I felt restless and went out for a walk by the sea. *(Sound of Tide)* There was a cool breeze, and the sea was loud with incoming tide. At dinner, I had arrogantly affronted a group of friends, and now I felt a lingering pain over the incident. I began washing the pain through my body, as if I were trying to cleanse myself with it. I did this until

I became aware that I was being observed by a naval military policeman. My behavior must have been startling. I had been cursing and stamping my feet and spitting on the ground. I dropped it and began walking again. I saw a young couple kissing in the shadow of a palm tree. Some distance away, a man was lying against the sea wall masturbating as he watched them. He took no notice of me, and I hurried away. I discovered that I was talking to myself in a loud voice. I stopped that and was composing myself when I was accosted by a leering, half-naked individual about sixty years old. He grasped my arm in a drunken stupor, his faded blue eyes hinting at some secret depravity. He told me, in broken Spanish, that he had just given his wife a good beating and proudly showed me her blood on his shirt.

Ah, don't hit me, don't hit me. Por favor!

Mangus I shoved him away, but he came back and clung onto me. His foul odor was overpowering. He kept insisting that he wanted to play with me. I pushed him from me, and, sick to my stomach, vomited onto the sand. Still, he would not let go. I lunged for a piece of driftwood and began swinging it at him. Drunkenly, he tried to elude the blows, not understanding the fury of my attack. At last, I clubbed him to the ground with a thumping blow to the head. He lay quietly on the sand. One of his eyes was hanging from his face on a thin strand of flesh.

Ayudame por favor!

Mangus I stood above him; my stick poised to hit him again should he move. I thought, "What a helplessly evil, stinking two-legged animal this is!" Down the beach were some young people sitting peacefully around a fire. I rushed at them with my stick. I wanted to destroy as many of these abominable creatures as I could...

(A red light flashes. Sound of foghorn.)

Lark Mangus?

Mangus I see myself, finally, in the mirror. Not at all what I thought. Nightmares. Always the same. Can't get there, can't find anything, can't get up, get down, go forward, laugh or cry. And the next day is lost.

Lark Do you hear something?

Mangus Yes, it's the tower on the bay.

Lark No, there's someone at the door. *(Banging)*

David Let me in! It's me, David!

Lark David!

David Yes! Let me in!

Mangus Shoot the motherfucker!

Lark No! Not that!

Mangus Fuck off!

Lark Go away!

(Sound of a Jaguar roar. Silence.)

Lark He's gone.

Mangus How do you know?

Lark I don't. He's right here. *(Double image: i.e., Screen and Stage)*

David For years I tried to unlock the secrets of this dead system. To bring it to life and light again. I studied the sacred numbers, but it was no use. Their meaning had been long forgotten. I was obedient to my parents, painfully shy, self-conscious from years of isolation. They could not tell me why the Sun was trembling across the sky becoming a black wormhole. I wanted to know. Perhaps with knowledge would come help. They said we had to go on, that it was not for us to know these things. Here and there I found crumbs of an Ancient Science based on studies of the Living Solar God. Time was passing and I couldn't fit the pieces together. All our light was the empty reflection of an electronic moon. I tried to concentrate, I wanted to feel the warmth of the Sun, even for a moment break the cycle of black gravity and night.

Lark What the fuck! Hit him with your club! *(Mangus does so. David has a strange fit, writhing and flailing about. Standing downstage left is the Jaguar Priest. He is relaxed and confident, handsome, dressed well in modern clothes.)*

Priest Drunken seizure are you. Lust of creation are you. Cock-macaw seizure are you. Deer seizure are you. Who is your tree? Who is your bush? What was your arbor? It is the place of Lady Needle of Blood, the Lady Remover of clotted blood? Removed is creation, removed is darkness, at the place where you vomited water and clotted blood. Macaw seizure! The snake monkey seizure! Erotic Monkey Seizure! Madness seizure! Cast them away, ye four gods, ye four *bacabs*, to fall in the place of the yellow Sun Eye! *(He grabs David by the neck and throws him to the ground. The club is luminescent with the colors of a jaguar. The Priest spins it and a whirling lamp of color appears above it.)* Cast them away, ye four gods, to the place of the Lady Mad Seizure Star. Four days he lay prostrate at the Lady Mad Seizure Star. There he bit the arm of the madness of creation, the madness of darkness. Then he licked the blood of the Maxcal plant. Then he licked the blood of the *Acantum,* the stone set up on a foundation. Then cast ye still the lust of creation, the lust of darkness, ye four gods, ye four *bacabs*. He would fall into the heart of the *Metnal*, the Underworld, at the place of the Father of Vigorous Enemy of fire, and of Lady Detrimental One who keeps closed the opening in the Earth. *(David vanishes. The Jaguar Priest picks up David's gleaming "power rock" from the floor and hands it to Mangus, along with a rolled document.)* Here is what you're looking for. You can go home now.

Mangus Where'd he go, David?

Priest: You can row out, if you want, if you feel like it, row out to his grave, tied to a cable in the far away sea—you can look down the cable into his memory. *(Exits)*

Lark What the fuck was that?

Mangus He gave us a scroll. From Ancient Mexico.

Lark We can go?

Mangus Where are the boys?

Lark In bed, where we left them.

Mangus Did you bow to the Beekeeper?

Lark Oh, fuck off with that shit, Mangus.

Mangus Okay. Let's go home.

A map, A close-up. A message. A descent. An image. A trail. A book. A rhythm. A pattern. A temple or a scroll.

Mangus A tattoo.

Lark Is what?

Mangus Insignia?

Lark For what?

Mangus I went on a killing spree. I got drunk. I bought guns and ammunition. I bought long guns. I went into a store, and I bought some guns and ammunition, no questions asked, long gun, and then I opened fire, I wanted revenge, bloody vengeance, too many people, shooters, I opened fire, I went on a spree, and I got drunk, and I started shooting. I enjoyed it. I was shooting the shit out of everything, people and dogs and babies, and horses and every fucking thing, I killed them all and I fucking enjoyed it. Guns and roses. I want to shoot. I'm an American. I shoot to kill. And I fucking enjoyed it.

Lark Shut up, Mangus. You're in the wrong movie. Pay attention. *(A series of sounds and comments as they travel back through time.)* Listen:

Break this cycle of black gravity and night... was hanging from his face on a thin strand of flesh. I stood above him... this is what happens when you get bombed. These are the bombs... the proportions are three, four, and five... and she wore re-jeweled earrings, and her lips were painted red, and there was red shadow around her narrow blue eyes... I would be unable to find my shoes. She herself had lost her heart, she said, and would never find it again... Would you ask David to come home? To— feed it every day with its food, the precious water, that is—human blood... far away, very far away... you think they'll answer me at Bellevue if I call them up on the phone?

Mangus Lark?

Mangus I've found the text. I think I've found it. I think David was referring to an old, twelve-sided canonical figure called The New Jerusalem. It's based on the dimensions of the Solar System. *(Reads: Projection.)* "The city had a wall great and high and twelve gates. And the foundations of the walls of the city were garnished with all manner of precious stones. And the twelve gates were twelve pearls; every several gates were one pearl. Amid the street of it, and on either side of the river was there the Tree of Life, which bore all manner of fruits, and yielded her fruit every month, and the leaves of the tree were for the healing of the Nations."

Lark Here we are.

Mangus Thoughts and prayers?

Lark Fuck off. Sun's out. Skies clear. Wake up the kids. We have a lot to tell them.

Mangus How 'bout the neighbors?

Lark Leave the neighbors alone, Motherfucker.

Mangus No problem. They were an event on the event horizon. Fun to watch.

Lark Stay out of it.

Mangus Definitely.

Lark And no alcohol.

Mangus Will you…? Sexual union today?

Lark Later, when the kids are sound asleep.

May their dreams forever keep.

Mangus "The beast with two backs?"

Lark NO. *(Out, to Audience)* I told you all about the demise of Mangus. One day he said was going up to the Washington Bridge. He's going to jump, he says. No, you're not, I say. Then, to spite me, he takes the subway up there anyway. They speak a foreign tongue, he tells me on the phone, and they're all Black, and there's a voodoo guy up here, he's a huge dude with a white mask on, a Jaguar mask, and he's waving me over, he wants to check me out. *(Pause)* That's the last we heard of Mangus the Motherfucker, live. Like I said earlier, we found him on the Bowery, eyes knocked out, mouth open, no teeth, pissed his pants, rolling in tar, on the street.

Wait a minute! What happened to his stick?

Mangus My stick is right here, Pal! *(Bangs it. Lights come on. To Lark)* You heard she got a restraining order?

Lark I'm not interested. *(To Audience:)* Of course, if it wasn't for all of you, he—Mangus—wouldn't be here at all.

Mangus *(Bows)* Thank you, very much.

Lark I meant all of us, Motherfucker. Not just you.

(The Actors all step forward and applaud the audience.)

END

THREE TABLES

A PLAY

Scene

Three tables in a restaurant or coffee shop, or just a club room. At one table are three friends, actors, Christen, Rodger, and Mike (40s and 50s). At another table, off to the side, sit Joe and Sol, older men, waiters or owners, or gents who think they own the place. A trio of other friends, also theater people, Margie, Don, and Casey, enter later and take a third table.

Production History

Three Tables premiered at The Zephyr Theater in Los Angeles in May of 2022.

Written and Directed by Murray Mednick
Produced by Racquel Lehrman

Scenic design: Joel Daavid
Costumes: Shon LaBlanc
Lighting Design: Azra King-Abadi
Compositions and sound design: John Zalewski

With: Richard Sabine, John Fantasia, Corey Rieger, Michael Uribes, Laura Liguori, Eric Stanton Betts, Raquel Cain and Dennis Renard

Lights up.

Christen I can have sex without having sex.

Rodger Bully for you.

Joe We were the first to use horses and we whacked them across the plain, the Savannah, the so-called origin of human life, in Africa.

Sol Not us.

Joe An idea, a concept.

Sol Wasn't us, Sol.

Rodger Sorry. I'm sorry I snapped at you.

Christen Why did you do it?

Rodger Someone had just told me to do something, and I was paralyzed by that.

Mike How so?

Rodger I don't know.

Mike Christen? How can you have sex without having sex?

Christen The vibe. I feel the vibe. But there's no penetration, no substances exchanged.

Joe While Death rode along with us. Was a part of us. What could we have been thinking? Law? Proverbs? Commandments?

Sol We are not people of the horse, Joe, we are people of the Book.

Christen A vibration exchanged.

Rodger Is that so?

Mike And the rest is fantasy and masturbation. Am I right?

Christen Right as rain.

Mike So what do you do?

Christen You get near a person and go from there, which is mainly standing, and holding your ground, and breathing.

Rodger You yelled at me, Chris. You did. "*Rodger! Don't pick up the chair!*"

Joe While the anti-Jew opens his mouth again, spitting murder and mayhem.

Sol What should we do?

Joe Get ready.

Sol How?

Joe Get ready now.

Christen Excuse me. Joe?

Joe *(Arriving)* Ma'am?

Christen My food is cold.

Joe Sorry.

Christen And it's not what I ordered.

Joe What did you order?

Christen Flank steak.

Joe That is flank steak.

Christen Take it back.

Joe Certainly, ma'am.

Christen And make sure it's hot.

Joe Same thing?

Christen Are you an idiot?

Joe Yes, ma'am.

Christen So don't stand here arguing with me.

Joe Be right back.

Christen I hope so. *(Joe returns to his station.)*

Rodger What was all that about?

Christen Food.

Rodger Can't you eat without eating.?

Christen Fuck off.

Rodger All that talk about love. Means nothing to you.

Christen Mainly nothing. True. I haven't thought about it, but that's all I know.

Rodger That's all you know?

Christen That's all I know, these days. I lie to myself. Tell stories. Fall in love.

Joe I'm gonna spit in her fucking food.

Sol Don't do that.

Joe I'm gonna spit in her food, or I'm gonna punch him in the head.

Sol Don't do that.

Joe I'm gonna kill the motherfucker.

Sol Serve her her flank steak.

Joe No, you do it.

Rodger Why did you yell?

Christen Sorry. What's wrong with you lately, Rodger?

Rodger Nothing. Nothing's wrong with me. Bad times are what's wrong with me.

Sol Arm ourselves. Build barricades.

Joe Too late. I'm an old man.

Sol An old hipster.

Joe Two old hipsters.

Sol That's what happened, Joe. Everybody laid down and took their punishment, and ate shit, and died.

Joe But I can still get it up.

Sol Give her her food.

Joe Let her wait.

Sol She'll complain.

Joe Let her wait.

Sol They'll fire you.

Mike Bad times is right.

Christen So I told you to pick up the freakin' chair.

Mike They're starting to round people up. Like the Brownshirts.

Rodger I'm not supposed to pick up chairs, Chris. I have bad knees.

Christen You can stand onstage alright.

Rodger I use painkillers and hang on to things.

Mike They throw them into vans and lock 'em up.

Christen Not good.

Rodger What did you say about falling in love, Chris?

Christen Too easily, is all.

Mike What about knowing your lines? That counts, too.

Christen I know my lines. Wouldn't you say so, Rodger?

Rodger No.

Sol Give it back to her. Same food.

Joe Yeah. *(Goes)* Here you are, ma'am.

Rodger 'Bout time.

Joe Thank you, ma'am.

Christen Much better.

Joe Yes, ma'am. *(Goes)*

Christen I always know my lines.

Rodger You're over the top.

Christen Fuck you.

Rodger Meanwhile, I'll have a chat with the waiters. Joe? We go back a long way. We were comrades in arms.

Mike Which side were you on, Joe?

Joe Get away from me you little shit, or I'll kill you with my bare hands. *(Pause)*

Mike Did you hear that?

Christen Shut up Mike.

Mike I know the owners.

Sol Stay cool, Joe.

Joe Yeah, back in the day. I wouldn't mind shooting guns, in the old days, or stomping people, or throwing grenades, but I can't run no more.

Sol Where to now, Joe?

Joe New York City?

Sol That's a fantasy. I like the idea, but a fantasy is what it is. We'll never make it there.

Joe I'll tell ya, Sol. I do look to the future now. My whole life I never looked ahead. With a positive attitude. And now I do.

Sol A little late for that, Joe.

Mike Rodger? What do you think?

Rodger Politics?

Mike Yeah.

Rodger Lie low.

Christen Lie low and learn your lines.

Rodger It's not only the lines. The things that happen onstage. Little touches. Looks. Attention paid. Listening to one another.

Christen I couldn't agree more. What we do is important.

Mike Yeah, yeah.

Christen You don't do shit, Mike.

Joe You think so? Sol? We couldn't make it in the Apple?

Sol Yes. You're right. Maybe we could. We have many brethren there.

Joe I look back, too. Had some good times. It ain't so bad. Ain't so bad at all. Remember Suarino, who jumped off the building on Broadway and survived?

Sol I do. Downtown.

Joe Now, he's a high-up in the *Hare Krishna* movement.

Sol LSD.

Joe Correct.

Sol A whole life chasing pharmaceuticals. Cannabis, hallucinogens. One doctor after another, one drugstore after another, one connection after another, one—I don't know. A lifestyle.

Christen You're a very strange person, Rodger.

Rodger Yes. I am. So what?

Christen Except maybe onstage.

Mike He's good. Onstage.

Christen Do you know exactly how you're strange?

Rodger No. You tell me.

Christen Like, for example, what's the doomsday here?

Rodger That's a line from the play.

Christen Doomed to what? I'm asking.

Rodger What's happening to the country.

Christen Come on. We're all worried.

Rodger Listen. I had this sudden impression of the audience. There they were, despite the horrors on the street, trying to pay attention. Eyes up. All sitting there quietly and everyone in their own heads, thinking thoughts and making up questions and answers like, "What does it all mean?", and all of them were going to die. For sure. That was my impression.

Mike That's what I saw, too, except plus the loneliness of everybody. And the fear. The apprehension.

Rodger Including us, Mike.

Christen Being lonely and wanting to be touched, wanting to be hugged and kissed.

Mike Wanting to get laid.

Christen What's wrong with that?

Mike Nothing. Totally normal.

Rodger You flirt too much, Christen.

Christen I can't believe you just said that, Rodger.

Joe What a strange thing it is, History. You think of the blood flowing up and down through Time like streams on a ball, or strings around the Earth, wrapping the Earth, and it has nothing to do with logic or reason.

Sol Just the murder impulse.

Joe Revenge of the Christians.

(Enter the three actors who sit at another table: number 3.)

Casey The drama.

Margie The theatricality.

Casey The loss.

Don The wait.

Casey The hope.

Don The dreaming.

Margie The imaginary.

Casey The idiot. *(Pause)*

Margie The murderous.

Christen Fuck you, Rodger.

Rodger Fuck you back.

Christen You've never been a normal person.

Rodger Thanks. Neither have you.

Christen Oh?

Rodger You liked that little kiss we had.

Christen Then, I did.

Rodger You flirt around too much. *(A pause—Christen gets up, stands, goes as if toward the bathroom, stops to say hello to Margie.)*

Christen Hi.

Margie Hi.

Christen I know you from the theater.

Margie Yeah. Good space.

Christen Definitely. Just wanted to say hello.

Margie Thanks for stopping by.

Christen You bet. *(Starts back to her table.)*

Sol *(To the newcomers)* Take a seat anywhere.

Margie Thank you!

Joe They did already, Sol.

Sol Where did we go wrong, Joe?

Joe Stiff-necked. Lost a major battle to the Arabs. Back in the day. Just think if we'd won.

Sol Then what?

Joe Then I don't know.

Sol Marched on the Persians or whoever it was, the Egyptians? The Greeks?

Joe Took prisoners and put them to work.

Sol No. Went on with the trade. The Ol' Silk Road.

Joe Hey. I like that. *(Christen returns to her table.)*

Mike Okay. Good. Sit down, Chris. I have an idea. Which is germane. I think.

Christen Which is what?

Mike Which is to make a "well." It's like a theater exercise I used to do. We rearrange the chairs so we imagine we're at a well. A well in the desert, a biblical well.

Rodger And then?

Mike We see what happens.

Rodger Stop with the fucking exercises, Mike.

Mike Let's try it. Chris?

Christen Okay. So, the table is like a well.

Mike Whatever. Let's make a triangle and *there* would be the well. Rodger?

Rodger Okay. There's the "well."

Mike Move the chairs a bit. *(They move the chairs, making a triangle.)*

Sol So why were they moving the chairs around?

Joe I don't know why.

Sol It's like the Absurdists.

Joe Absurd. Definitely.

Rodger What happened was, Chris, it was a moment of not knowing what to do, or who I was, because you yelled my name, and I was spooked. I felt paralyzed and blank, because I knew I had snapped at you, and I hadn't wanted to. *It* snapped.

Christen I never said anything about it, Rodger.

Rodger Let's drop it.

Mike Let's look at the "well."

Christen *(Pointing)* There's the well.

Sol As I was saying, as I said, so they got meekly onto buses and trains and went where they went, of which I will not speak. Only of revenge, will I speak.

Joe Seems far-fetched, to me. Seems like there was only one way to go, and so that's the way it went.

Sol The Europeans, especially the idiots in the East, they walked by Synagogues on a Friday night—they heard singing and happiness, and it made them mad.

Casey Do we know these people?

Margie Not really.

Joe I was talking to so and so and that's what he said. On the rise. Anti-Semitism on the rise. In France.

Sol All over. What are people? They get an idea in their heads, and they have to execute? Swords! Thundering hooves across the plain! Blood and booty!

Joe I think we have to wait on these people.

Sol Let's give 'em a minute.

Rodger This acting company walks in and all of them are going to die. *(Pause)* I think I'll tell them.

Christen Leave them be, Rodger.

Rodger We know some of them.

Mike No, we don't. We just share the space.

Christen It's not normal to say things like that. To strangers.

Casey Anyway, facing front all the time. I don't know how I feel about that. It's not natural.

Don It's Vaudevillian.

Casey And the timing thing.

Margie You get your head right by knowing that right away.

When to speak, when to move. *Pause.*

Casey Not a second too late, or too soon.

Don Right away.

Casey Right on time.

Margie It's mixing shit up.

Casey Say again?

Margie Never mind. *El directeur.*

Casey I know what you mean.

Margie I think that's the problem. Plus what's happening in the street. Now you see 'em, now you don't.

Mike Reminds me of those vacation calls about the phony vacation package—they are preying on people with these vacation package and boat rides, it's the most evil thing, preying on the old and unemployed with lies and possibilities behind the lies, and it's all allowed by American justice, such as it is.

Christen Don't fret. Hang up the phone.

Rodger I get it, I do get it. But I have to admit. I get the calls.

Christen Don't answer the calls.

Joe Robbery and murder—they get a kick out of it. And if you have a little booze or amphetamine, all the better. Rock and roll.

Sol I've never told anyone, but I hate that stuff. I hate whadyacallit, too—hip hop. Rap. Stupid. I'm a Thelonius Monk, Bud Powell type of person.

Joe Bully for you.

Sol What can you do? What'll happen to all the intellectuals?

Joe Dead as doornails.

Sol Or end up as waiters, like us. We got like a rock group here and this looks like the Actors' Humane Society. A house full of actors.

Joe *HaShem* bless us all.

Sol Amen.

Don This fucking country is going to the wolves and the pigs, the hustlers and the cons.

Casey They must succeed sometimes, with the old and the horny, the old and the shaky. My parents. Can't remember if they bought a boat ride to Timbuktu or the Bermuda Triangle, or what.

Margie We weren't talking about that.

Don What were we talking about? The street. You brought it up yourself.

Margie Stagecraft.

Casey Timing. Interesting stuff.

Margie I was just thinking, loneliness is a terrible thing, and then to be preyed upon. A body, a woman's body, it has all these parts, and they have to be touched. It's just a shame what happens, a woman alone and untouched, it's a fucking shame.

Don Timing. You can't teach it.

Casey But what is it coming to, when you get a phone call in the middle of the day about a trip you bought to Trinidad and Tobago? What is that?

Don He's got a point there.

Casey Or they're selling you tickets to a phony dance. I made that up, but you know what I mean.

Don Call one of the waiters. They're just sitting there bull-shitting.

Margie Waiter! *(Joe rises and goes to her.)*

Joe Yes, ma'am?

Margie Three vodka martinis please. We're on a break.

Joe You got it. *(Goes)*

Rodger Something snapped. I apologize.

Christen And you were trembling.

Rodger I was trembling?

Christen Yes. It's those little pills you take.

Rodger Those are steroids.

Christen Steroids.

Rodger Yes.

Mike Why do you take steroids?

Rodger You know why—it's my knees.

Christen They make you shake.

Rodger Oh.

Mike Not onstage.

Rodger Thank God.

Don So, as I was saying...

Margie What images that brings up! I can tell you that! Lined up against the wall, hoping some fathead will be able to say a whole sentence. In your ear. While he fumbles with your dress. We hit the boards and then we hit the bars.

Don Show biz!

Margie We got one going here—like a round of golf or a game of Horse. Or jousting a joust. Must have been what happened with old Will Shakespeare. Jam sessions and iambic pentameter and a lot to rhyme with.

Don Sounds right. That's what he wants, the director.

Margie Yes, it's a verbal celebration, a round, so let's don't stop now, or we'll all fall down.

Casey Good, Marge!

Don Don't stop.

Margie Pass Go.

Don Slide home.

Margie Oh, my. Sounds good and feels good.

Don We're on our way.

Casey It's not a vacation package though.

Don Not today.

Margie Old bodies in the throes of desire and open laughter!

Casey Yeah!

Joe *(Preparing the drinks.)* Actors. I got 'em, Sol.

Sol What can you do? What'll happen to all the actors and intellectuals?

Joe Dead as doornails, like was said.

Sol They killed a third of the Jewish gene pool already.

Joe We're not supposed to think that way.

Sol Genes. What are Genes? Strands of DNA. Science. It's Adam, or whoever it was, naming things again.

Joe I'm on my way.

Margie What are we made of? Flesh and yearnings of the heart and the delusions of the mind. Something like that. And we get crinkled and wrinkled and bullshitted and conned. What's it mean, a "happy old age." You'd think sex would have something to do with that, but apparently it doesn't.

Casey Thank you, sir.

Joe You're welcome. *(Goes)*

Casey And I was thinking, "sex is dirty," but it's not.

Don The Sages said the sex apparatus is right next to the shithole.

Casey I don't want to think that way.

Margie It's fun if you can get some of the grunts and groans out of the way.

Don Good luck with that.

Margie Take it slow.

Don Take it easy.

Margie Take it as it comes.

Don Take it woke.

Casey Take a shower.

Don Hey!

Rodger Onstage I'm not like that. Onstage it all goes away, and I fly the magic carpet.

Christen But that's not what I'm getting at.

Rodger What are you getting at?

Christen It's how you are in general.

Rodger I have no idea. Well, I have some idea.

Christen We know that. You're odd.

Rodger Odd?

Christen Maybe that's the wrong word.

Rodger I wouldn't have thought, "Odd."

Christen No?

Rodger No.

Christen Nuts, maybe. Maybe you're nuts.

Rodger I feel hurt by that, Christen.

Christen I'm sorry. Don't think about it.

Rodger Don't think about it? *(Pause)*

Don I'm looking out at mankind, and I am not encouraged.

Margie I might add that my libido is not what it once was.

Casey At least you have some left.

Don In the imagination.

Margie So easily deceived we are, by our thoughts and feelings.

Don Without which, what are we?

Casey Specks.

Don Dust.

Casey Nothing.

Margie A vibration?

Sol What a strange concept, when you think about it. You could say, since it already happened, that it's happening now.

Joe Funny way to put it, Sol. The Christians. In the South. Their fucking attitude.

Sol It's in the soil, it's in the air we breathe.

Joe It's in their heads.

Sol Monotheism? Is that the cause?

Joe I don't think so, and we probably got that from the Egyptians.

Joe We were on the edge of the Roman Empire in the first century B.C. They don't like the competition. Is what it is.

Sol Survival.

Joe But who knows? They don't know anything but what they find in the sand.

Sol Sand?

Joe Sand.

Casey He wants us to remember the dead. Traditions. The ancestry.

Don Raises the question what remains of the remains?

Margie We may never know.

Casey You never know.

Don We might find out.

Margie We might have some purpose, being a link between the Earth and the Sun, like the Egyptians may have thought, some kind of service, so they wrapped their mummies—sorry, don't know where I was headed with that. I think about it. I wonder about it. What actually happened, and why did they do that?

Don Perhaps the question of memory and the blood.

Margie No, they tried to keep the body intact. That's how I understand it. Wrapped and sealed.

Don Why?

Margie I don't know why. *(Pause)*

Don They're trying now to take away the science, the truth, the facts that make the science. I don't know how to say it. It's sad.

Rodger I grew up among the lower classes. We don't feel like you people. We don't feel equal. We wonder if we belong.

Christen Don't worry about it. You're smart. You're even good-looking. But you're getting a belly. I'd stop drinking if I were you.

Rodger I'll never stop drinking. Why? Because it relaxes the mind, Christen. And don't tell me what to do.

Christen Don't tell me what to do, either. I do what I want.

Rodger That's for sure.

Christen I change my mind.

Joe Memory and the blood.

Sol Is what?

Joe The Jewish version of immortality. I overheard them talking over there.

Sol See if they want another drink.

Joe Okay. *(Approaches)*

Margie I'm thinking of menstruation now and the monthly bleeding. By association. I'm free of that these days, thank God.

Joe Can I get you people something?

Casey No, thanks. *(Joe goes.)* Memory and blood. To be remembered, to pass on the genes. The bloodline and the Word.

Don No genes for me. None passed on. Does that mean I'm cut off? That the progeny is gone? Vacant. Like I was never here in the first place? You can say that about all the world. The Earth is bleeding. Oceans choking on plastic.

Casey The Egyptians—sorry. I forget now.

Joe They hate us because we're smart.

Sol Like I used to say to whatshisname, we have talent and the women like sex.

Joe Not all of them.

Sol Intelligence and we fuck a lot. That used to really bug him. Jack was his name. I'd become the little Jewish clown to him. It's an identity now in my head. I used to really get his goat. The Jews are smarter. The Jews are more talented. The Jews get laid a lot.

Joe You liked that?

Sol Yes. Not really. Lots of problems there. You're like the inside of the outside.

Joe I didn't get that.

Sol You're on the outside looking in.

Joe Oh. I see.

Rodger Vodka is a boon to mankind.

Mike Right.

Christen Why?

Mike Well…

Christen Not you!

Rodger Okay, let's move on.

Christen It muddles the mind.

Joe Sad commentary on the progress of Man.

Sol You could have a penetration and wind up with a cretin or a brain-damaged imbecile, at our age.

Joe Good point.

Sol Who would want that?

Casey I was saying, the Egyptians knew how to organize, but the Jews did them one better.

Don Here he goes with the Jews again.

Casey They had a God who could visit with plagues. Who could blow their minds.

Margie You can't do better than that.

Casey No.

Joe Funny, to look ahead when there ain't much there to come anymore.

Sol I'd say so. I'll go and check on the table.

Joe What about the rock and rollers?

Sol They're done.

Joe Check anyway.

Sol Okay. *(Goes)*

Rodger That tears it.

Christen Look at the well, Rodger.

Rodger No, you look at it.

Christen I am looking at it.

(Sol approaches table number 3.)

Sol Another drink?

Casey No, thanks.

Margie I think I'll have one. *(Looks at Casey)* No, never mind.

Casey Your name is Sol, right?

Joe Right.

Casey Thanks, a lot, Sol.

Sol You're welcome. *(Goes)*

Don And they knew about vibrations.

Margie The Egyptians or the Jews?

Don Maybe both. And you?

Margie Me, what?

Don Thoughts?

Sol *(Returning)* Everything's copacetic. You like country?

Joe The music?

Sol Yeah.

Joe No. Why? I don't identify with it. I don't feel like an American. I'm second generation in this country, so I'm just not into it.

Sol I agree with that. I'm the same.

Don Margie?

Margie I'm thinking about the many relationships. I haven't thought about it in a while. I was lucky. I'm thinking about it because the younger ones, you know, they run into trouble with money and drugs, and screwing around, just like us, apparently, so I'm looking back, except in those days it seemed fraught, you know, with consequence. And we were at war at the time, to boot, and dead soldiers were arriving, in coffins, and hard hats attacked us, in the good old American way.

Joe It's either that or assimilate, or convert, or pack it in.

Sol Pack it in.

Joe Yeah. Forget about it.

Sol Stop eating.

Joe I can see that.

Sol The world is the World.

Joe Right.

Sol The universe is the Universe.

Joe Everything is Everything, as we used to say.

Mike Just listen to these guys...

Christen Shut up, Mike.

Mike No, you shut up.

Christen I don't need help from you, Mike.

Mike Okay, okay. Let's play. The Well. "Actors must learn to play."

Rodger "Who said so?"

Mike "I heard it on the radio."

Rodger That's a quote. From our play.

Christen I know.

Don Vibrations?

Casey What is it with the vibrations?

Margie That was not put right. Just so you know.

Don The Ancients knew about vibration. Everyone knew. That and alchemy, too.

Margie Bad things happened, and they keep on fucking happening, and the idiots keep on singing *God Bless America.*

Mike Let's move the chairs around.

Rodger We did that already.

Mike Yeah, but a lot of time has passed.

Rodger What's the problem with that?

Mike Not a problem. Just move 'em an inch.

Christen Okay. *(They adjust their chairs a little.)* Let's play The Well.

Rodger I don't want to play.

Christen Petulant.

Rodger I don't feel like playing.

Mike Then don't.

Christen You've never been normal, Rodger.

Rodger Thanks. But fuck you, too.

Mike Hey, waiter!

Joe What?

Mike Can we have another round here?

Joe Coming right up!

Mike Thank you!

Margie Yeah, they didn't like who I was, ultimately, or something. I'm not sure what they were getting at. I liked to drink and smoke? I liked the news on TV? What? Not enough confidence or mojo? What?

Don You may never know.

Margie It's right there under my nose. A fault or a weakness. A shortcoming, as they say. A certain partiality. A certain attitude. Selfishness.

Don All of the above.

Margie I'm not kidding.

Casey I know you're not. Excuse me. *(Gets up and goes Off.)*

Don I know you're not, believe me. It's not like I don't have my so-called issues, like losing my temper and yelling at people, and taking advantage.

Margie Practice not being a wise guy for a while, and the whole thing becomes a performance.

Don You think so?

Margie Yes. I'm thinking about loneliness and touch at the moment. I think it all comes from the vibration motif.

Joe Quite a crew over there.

Sol The universe is the Universe.

Joe Young.

Sol It is what it is.

Joe Whatever it is. They should be careful.

Sol They don't have to dress all in black and behave strangely amidst the population of strangers.

Joe Who's that?

Sol The religious. The fanatics. They make us look bad.

Joe People are used to it.

Sol They stand out.

Joe They'll be rounded up in the street.

Sol God, I hope not.

Joe And not just them.

Rodger (*Moving his chair*) How's this?

Mike Different view.

Christen You experiment too much with your mind.

Mike You fuck with your head too much, Rodger.

Rodger Who says so?

Christen Drugs and the mind. You believe drugs effect the mind.

Rodger They do. For better or worse.

Christen One must guard the doors of perception.

Rodger Indeed. One must guard the doors.

Mike The idea is that the artifact is the thing itself, not a representation.

Rodger How is that related, Mike?

Christen That's like saying the world is a museum.

Rodger I don't know what that means either, Christen.

Mike Right.

Christen Who said that?

Mike I did.

Christen I have no idea what you meant.

Mike Right.

Christen You're too stupid, really, Mike, to follow what I'm saying.

Rodger No, he isn't.

Christen He is. He doesn't see them coming.

Margie Like, it's having someone in the room. Anyone. But especially someone who cares about you, who has some feeling. Just their physical presence. I think that's a very big thing. Just someone being there.

Don The vibe.

Margie Yeah. That's what I'm saying.

Joe And us? They'll find our names and addresses.

Sol There'll be a knock on the door.

Joe Like those "shithole" countries.

Sol With shithole dictators.

Joe And all I wanted to do was write poetry.

Sol Good luck with that.

Joe And become moderately famous.

Sol Of course.

Joe Looked up to and respected. Highly thought of.

Sol I'm a would-be scientist. We'd be in it for the money, basically.

Joe Oh, come on.

Sol Status, maybe.

Joe Status.

Sol And there's a little idealism there. New thoughts, discoveries. The nature of matter, of gravity. And so on.

Joe Einstein.

Sol He was a believer, you know.

Joe Yes, but he got out quick.

Sol Of what?

Joe Religion.

Sol I don't know what to think. I'm too old to fight.

Joe What's the count, by the way?

Sol Fuck the count.

Joe What's the count, Sol?

Sol Twenty-seven.

Joe Thank you.

Sol Dinner.

Joe Right.

Mike You see it all the time in the movies. You see it on television. You see it in plays.

Rodger See what? Say again?

Mike That what's happening is not what's happening, but a stand-in for something else. Like in a dream.

Rodger But I don't see Life as a dream right now. Not now.

Christen Why not?

Rodger I can make the mental move toward Reality. But I suppose dreams are also useful.

Christen You're always like that—dreaming.

Rodger Not always. Sometimes I know what I'm doing. It all seems the same to me. You get up and do what you have to do, and that's that.

Christen Eat, shit, and die.

Mike Right. They're rounding people up in the streets now. In unmarked uniforms, like the Brownshirts.

Christen Right. You said that. We ought to sneak it into the play.

Mike I think we should.

Christen Write something, Rodger.

Rodger Me?

Don It's something of the utmost importance. So you think ahead, you look forward, you're mindful of the situation. You take care, you consider.

Margie But it's not like making a catalogue, either. Or an album. Or a diary. I was going to say, "You listen, you pay attention." So what are you going to do? You do what you do. And then you look back and you say, "Why the fuck did I do that? And *that* way? What was I thinking?"

Don Yeah. Fear, Marge. Fear.

Sol The count. All we worry about is the count.

Joe Why worry? The count is the Count. *(Casey comes back from the bathroom.)*

Don The worst thing is anticipating the worst. The sense of dread. You're setting yourself up for the inevitable future disaster.

Margie You play your role. You learn your part. No, you choose your part, and you learn your lines, and you play the part, and so on. What I mean is, you've read the script, and now you have to play it out.

Casey I don't know about the choice there. Is there a choice? I bailed. Basically, I bailed. I thought I was making a decision, but one day I found myself on the outside looking in, and the door never opened again. So I moved on—heroically. No, actually, I was struck through the heart. Speared. It was like being killed.

Don I know this fellow—he believes in Free Will. He says God leaves it up to us. Somehow this doesn't jibe with mass murder.

Casey Is that what's bothering you?

Don No.

Casey What's bothering you?

Don He's too far away to do anything, tantamount to not being there. Not your friend, God himself.

Casey Is that how you see it?

Don That's how I see it. Take note they searched the skies and found a hole, a Black Hole. They have a picture now of something like Reality, where the gravity is so intense everything vanishes into it. Even light.

Sol What about the family?

Joe They're all Gentiles.

Sol How did that happen?

Joe I'm not sure, really. I was always attracted. The wind blows the sand around. And you?

Sol What?

Joe Family?

Sol I don't know what to do. I have to think about it. Do you hide? Do you run? Do you run and hide?

Rodger Talking about plays, it's not what you think. It's not like a *Bad Day In L.A.*

Mike It's not like that at all. They bad-mouth you. It's like a bad day in L.A. for real.

Rodger Yeah, and cheap, cheap with the dough, with the claudits.

Christen The claudits?

Rodger Yeah, you know, like on the internet, like in the texts.

Christen What texts?

Rodger Any texts.

Christen Come on!

Rodger Okay, forget that, the emails and the documents. People are saying what the fuck, friends of yours. You think they care about you, that they give a fuck, otherwise the money?

Christen No.

Mike Well, there you go, big shot.

Margie People have things on their minds. Living their lives.

Don Yeah. Yeah, like he thinks he's something. Big Ego. Acts tough, or needy. Depending.

Margie Don?

Don On the situation, the requirements.

Casey Like what?

Don Like I don't give a shit what.

Casey Okay.

Sol I feel like we're back in the twentieth century.

Joe We are far as I'm concerned.

Sol But I'm sad to hear all that.

Joe Yeah, wake up finally why don't you.

Margie I'm glad, because I can be myself, by myself.

Casey You need others. You can't be without others. It's a problem for you.

Margie It's a problem. I'm trying to see it. I'm trying to be nice.

Casey It's not like that, and it's late in the day. And the Earth has moved its axis. Or haven't you heard. So I'd get around to it one day, though I really don't know there's much to do, to actually do.

Christen What is love then?

Mike Round and round, nothing personal involved, I can tell you that.

Christen Thank you, Mike.

Rodger You want to think of forces, big forces. *(Pause)* Now I'm silent. I have nothing more to say. But I thought you should know. What's what. And stop with the dreaming. The false impression you have.

Christen I see that.

Mike No, you don't.

Christen I feel it.

Margie They know nothing.

Casey We're here now, and then, soon, we vanish.

Margie So, immortality is our chief concern, as we were saying earlier.

Casey What must that be, but a fine vibration? So fine as to be invisible?

Don That, too, can be swallowed by the Hole. No matter how fine, no matter how visible or not, it is the absolute vanishing point. As you can see on the Kabbalah Tree of Life, above the Highest is Nothing, below the Lowest is Nothing. Rabbis have been twisting their heads over that one.

Margie You associate the Black Hole with Nothing?

Don I do. This gives me no cheer.

Margie But it is not Nothing. It is Gravity. Where there is ostensibly no Time, or time going backwards. And yet I can touch the Present from time to time. What is that?

Don The Present has two ends, both nothing. Here, now, gone. The Present is the vibration of nothing. Not quite what it's cracked up to be.

Joe Three times I was almost murdered. Once with a large knife on East Fourth Street. Once in Santa Fe. Once by a big junkie with a large door key. Once an O.D.

Sol Who wants to hear about it?

Joe Not me. Just remembering. Stupid, really.

Sol Welcome to America.

Joe Land of the free.

Sol A plutocracy is what it is, Joe.

Margie So what do we serve? What's the point?

Don God sees himself through Man. Or knows Himself through Man.

Casey And what is the Black Hole?

Margie Gravity. It's the effect of mass. Bodies. I was thinking of Love, I was thinking of Love.

Casey How did the Black Hole become Love?

Margie I was talking sex, but I think I meant *love*. I'm not sure. *Love. Love* in the Universe. Can you fathom that? I can't mention names, but that's what I was talking about, an expression of *love*, a vibe, we could both feel it. And the others too, all the others, the touches and feelings and thoughts—all *love*.

Mike Don't try to change anything, Rodger. It's perfectly alright.

Rodger So I can't contribute?

Mike Go ahead.

Christen It's all about the drugs, isn't it?

Rodger Is it?

Christen Like the steroids, and God knows what else. That's why you tremble. That's why you paralyze.

Rodger I don't know about that. My brain freezes up and I'm in emotional pain. And nobody gives a shit. That's what gets me. It's not that you don't know. You know, you just don't give a rat's ass. And that's what hurts me, and paralyzes me, freezes me.

Mike You're depressed.

Rodger I'm not depressed.

Christen We all have our own problems, you know.

Rodger Yeah, yeah. It's like the cards I have—are the cards I have. They are not symbolic of an inner life or coincdence with an inner anything. They're my real cards.

Christen Who could follow that?

Rodger Just one more thing.

Christen What's that?

Rodger They were digging up the bones. Right?

Mike So what?

Rodger So I can't buy any of that. I can't buy it. Like my own bones, arthritic bones in my knees, in my back—

Mike In your brain.

Rodger Not in my brain. In my body, when we kissed—

Christen We didn't kiss, we touched lips.

Rodger —The bones. Listen "Even when I was standing near her, and we felt the vibe, my bones hurt, I was aware of my bones, and the thoughts came of the vanishing bones of the dead, though they dig 'em up and we make history out of it." That's it and that's all, so where's the *love,* where's the fucking *Love*? I'm asking you.

Mike *(Aside)* It's up your ass.

Joe The only way out is *up.*

Sol Great. A Jewish spaceship. We'll colonize Mars.

Joe If they don't have anti-Semites there already.

Sol What's that?

Joe If they don't have anti-Semites there already. Hidden under the rocks. Envy and greed, buried on Mars. Under the rocks on Mars.

Sol Get serious.

Joe Under the sand. Blown here and there by the solar wind.

Sol Stop now.

Christen You've always been not normal, Rodger.

Rodger Okay. You've said that. Thank you.

Christen In the sense that you're not functioning with a complete ego. You've said so yourself.

Rodger Did I?

Christen Yeah.

Rodger I don't even know what that means.

Christen No ego and low self-esteem.

Rodger No. I said *big* ego and low self-esteem.

Christen Nothing about the Brownshirts.

Rodger No.

Margie And then there was a knock on the door. Loud and crisp. Knock, knock, knock. Definite, loud. I woke up from a nightmare, and then the *knock*. It's very frustrating, because I can't remember the nightmare, and it woke me up. It woke me up and then the *knock*. It sounded absolutely real. So I sit up and I say, *oh shit*, it's a fucking knock on the door and it's three o clock in the morning, it's some fucking Mexican teenager, or some bum, or a *Chabad* mafioso, so I turn on the lamp, *oh shit I hope nobody's out there*, but I put on my robe and I sneak to where I can take a look where nobody can see me, and there's nobody there. A part of me is expecting to see a hulk out there waiting to kill me, but it was not to be. This has happened to me before, when I was almost murdered, years ago, by a Latino on PCB or whatever it is, dust that hallucinates you, in L.A., while I was watching the Sparks on TV, and I fought him off—but there was nobody there last night and I saw myself creeping around as though there was. It seems like a dream now, like an extended nightmare, as I crawl back in bed. I hope I can sleep now. But that's not all. It's like I was watching the entire episode, detached, as if it was two of us there. Watching. And I wonder. I wonder what happened to my dream, and I wonder about death, what happens when we die.

Mike Those were the cards you were dealt. You see the contradiction there? It would make anybody shake.

Rodger You stay out of this, you.

Mike *(Gesturing)* Full house. Aces and kings.

Christen What did that mean?

Mike You missed it, Christen.

Rodger There's no point to any of that. None. It's some sort of pretend meaning. Which is the real reason. Because I don't believe in all that bullshit, existential or otherwise, religious or otherwise, political or otherwise.

Mike What do you believe in?

Rodger Nothing. Absolutely nothing.

Casey And the bones. Scientists picking at our teeth. Tossing our skulls around. I mean, I'm looking at my body right now and I hear my heartbeat, and I snort and I have to take a leak, I'm a complete slave to these biological processes.

Margie That makes sense. I can understand that. We women have our periods and the blood washes through us like we are mere instruments of nature, vessels for the rushing of blood and liquids and God knows what else. We're being flushed. We have no choice in the matter.

Rodger So what did this guy mean, your friend, about freedom of choice?

Christen I don't know. He thinks God created the Universe.

Mike Okay.

Rodger No one had told me about the death of his mother. So I was acting normally. Then I realized. It was like walking through a glass door. It happens. I knew something was wrong, but I didn't know what it was. Affects trust in the company.

Christen So, what are you saying?

Rodger I don't trust anybody no more.

Christen I don't know if any of it was intentional.

Rodger Even more telling. Talk about being on the outside looking in.

Christen You didn't know the woman.

Rodger No. Because everyone was looking at me like I was a stranger. Some people didn't even talk to me. Hundreds of meetings, rehearsals I've had with you. And then I walk smack into the door.

Christen So what are you saying?

Rodger I don't know. Whacked.

Sol The Philosophers don't tip very well. Go figure.

Joe And you? You're a waiter, and you yell at waiters.

Sol I don't know why I do that.

Joe You want to see things done right, that's all. Look. They're getting ready to leave.

Sol By the way. Make sure you have money and I.D. At all times.

Joe Absolutely right.

Sol At all times.

Joe I hear you there.

Sol And think of a way out. The people who left early, in Europe, their lives were saved.

Joe Right. Meanwhile, we have to go on living.

Sol Lemme ask you—why?

Joe Why not?

Sol Indeed. Why not?

Rodger The American Dream, it's a con.

Mike So why do they all want to come here?

Rodger This is where the money is. For the moment.

Christen People have to live.

Rodger The End is near, my dear.

Christen Don't call me, "Dear."

Don Let's go.

Margie Leave a tip.

Casey I left a tip.

Don Let's go.

Margie Leave a tip.

Casey I left a tip.

Margie It's not enough.

Casey It's enough.

Don In six days of the Bible, or the Big Bang and the subservient, I mean subsequent, tumult. Stars and planets and flying rocks.

Margie A tiny dot of Conscious Will?

Don God?

Casey Something must come all the way down to us. Like the *Logos*.

Don Right here. Now.

Margie Let's go. *(They start to exit.)*

Rodger An ace is an ace and a king is a king.

Mike Right.

Christen Why don't you write something?

Rodger I don't feel like it anymore. I feel blank. Empty. That's what happens in these stupid meetings.

Christen We need to come up with something. Mike here is trying to come up with the cards thing, the representation idea, so maybe that's a start.

Rodger I kind of agree with that.

Christen Agree with what?

Rodger This. The thing is representative of itself. It is what it is.

Joe Love our wives and family. Visit the graves of our ancestors.

Sol Say a prayer. Recite a *midrash.*

Joe Put on some music. Try Beethoven.

Sol Okay. *(Music)*

Joe Nice.

Sol Yes.

Joe Here's a thought "Life as a manifestation of an energy, the source of which is unknown." And energy cannot die.

Sol Are you saying, "That is the nature of things, the reality of which we speak, unknowingly, of Life?"

Joe What an idiot. I can't talk to you.

Sol The ghost of Samuel Beckett haunts us, Joe. Because all the questions about the Truth—they're all the same.

Christen So tell us please what's bothering you.

Rodger You didn't tell me about Sandy's mother's death. Why didn't you tell me?

Christen I don't know why. I think it was merely accidental.

Rodger It says so much of how the cast thinks of me. The opposite of what I thought myself, needless to say.

Mike Well, don't react.

Rodger Is that all you can say? I have to react. I'm a person.

Christen No one meant anything by it, Rodger.

Rodger Yes, they did.

(Table number 3 at the exit.)

Margie So, I don't see the point of the whole thing.

Casey No?

Margie No. I think we should raise hell and quit.

Casey What do you mean?

Margie What I said. Raise hell and quit.

Don Now?

Casey Hit the street?

Margie Hit it.

Don Now?

Margie Now. *(They exit)*

Sol There goes that party.

Joe *Zie Gezunt.*

Sol Small tip.

Joe Theater people.

Sol They're up to something.

Joe The whole world is up to something.

Sol Rioting in the street.

Joe A virus in the air. Fungi in the ground. Clouds full of bad fantasies.

Sol You're out there, Joe. Made of fat, by the way.

Joe What is?

Sol The virus.

Joe Who told you that?

Sol The television.

Joe Hate, envy, bloodlust, lies. Oh, what the fuck.

Rodger I have to say, there's something sinister about the whole thing. There is. Something sinister. It's the sense that history has lost its shoes.

Mike Wow.

Rodger So history is floating an inch above the Earth, like a cloud or like the ocean.

Mike What an image!

Rodger My father used to lie down under the water at Coney Island. He'd pop up and say, "Look, I was in the sky!" We all laughed. He wasn't all wrong, because the ocean met the sky on the horizon.

Christen What was your mother doing?

Rodger My mother was nervous. Pitter-pattered around, worrying about the hard-boiled eggs. Pretzels and Pepsis. I had siblings at the time. I don't know what they were doing. Me, I used to hide under the shade of the boardwalk. It was so crowded on the beach you only had room for your body. It was so hot in the city we slept on the fire escape or the roof.

Mike Nobody was talking about mass murder at the time.

Christen No.

Rodger Not that I remember.

Christen No.

Mike Nobody talked about the Shoah until the seventies. Out of shame, out of despair and humiliation. Where were you, Rodger?

Rodger Central Brooklyn. Very few people spoke English. They spoke with shivs and billy-clubs and rocks. You could ride the trolley all the way to the Navy Yard. Mainly I hung out in alleys.

Sol Let's blow this joint and head for France.

Joe No. Too much anti-Semitism.

Sol The food is good.

Joe Definitely.

Sol Israel.

Joe No. Too much right-wing. Think of All that has come before us, and of the future, where you've got these lying sonsofbitches, how do we lock them up, for Eternity—Hell, in other words?

(A loud knocking at the door. Christen stands. It stops, resumes, stops, Christen sits down. The scene below repeats, as though happening for the first time.)

Rodger *I have to say, there's something sinister about the whole thing.*

Christen *There is. Something sinister. It's the sense that History has lost its shoes.*

Mike *Wow.*

Rodger *So History is floating an inch above the Earth, like a cloud or like the ocean.*

Christen *I didn't get that.*

Rodger *My father used to lie down under the water at Coney Island. He'd pop up and say, "Look, I was in the sky!" We all laughed. He wasn't all wrong, because the ocean met the sky on the horizon.*

Christen *What was your mother doing?*

Rodger *My mother was nervous. Pitter-pattered around, worrying about the hard-boiled eggs. Pretzels and Pepsis. I had siblings at the time. I don't know what they were doing. I used to hide under the shade of the Boardwalk. It was so crowded on the beach you only had room for your body. It was so hot in the city we slept on the fire escape, or the roof.*

Mike *Nobody was talking about mass murder at that time.*

Christen *No.*

Rodger *Not that I remember.*

Christen *No.*

Mike *Nobody talked about the Shoah until the seventies. Out of shame, out of despair and humiliation. Where were you, Roger?*

Rodger *Central Brooklyn. Very few people spoke English. They spoke with shivs and billy-clubs and rocks. You could ride the trolley all the way to the Navy Yard. Mainly I hung out in alleys. (Pause)*

Mike Can we get back to the main topic now?

Rodger Fuck the meeting. Fuck the play. Fuck the break. Fuck the topic.

Christen We were having a personal crisis. A Rodger event.

Mike And remember, we have a "*well*" now.

Christen Let's throw her into the well.

Mike Throw her into the well.

Rodger Who?

Christen The woman fetching water.

Mike Why?

Christen No reason. An exercise.

Mike Okay.

Christen Rodger?

Rodger Miming or mentating?

Christen The mind. Think it. *(A silence)*

Sol People will do anything. Just tell them often enough. What is that? Like monkeys. Chimpanzees.

Joe B.C. On the Roman border. Salonika.

Sol Is what?

Joe Hatred for the *suppliers*, the army. The army and the barbarians.

Christen The lies I tell myself. *(Pause)* The fantasies. I get emotionally attached, and then I believe in them. And then the truth comes as a shock. That's what I like about acting. It's not me.

Mike It is you.

Christen No, I'm not lying. Onstage. Hopefully.

Rodger May I intervene?

Christen Of course.

Mike Why throw this woman into the well?

Christen I don't know why. It's one of my Christens, shouting in the sky.

Rodger May I?

Mike Go.

Rodger There's no representation for what I'm trying to say. I was a boy, then. Now, you got to get ready and come clean. But I feel a barrier in my chest, reminds me of a subway platform and a train zooming into the platform.

Mike Wow.

Rodger My father never knew how to ask for help, even though he needed it, badly. He was a lot like I am now.

Christen Ask for help and you might get it.

Rodger Help!

Christen Here comes the train. Get on the train.

(Loud sound of subway going by)

Rodger No, but I have a question.

Mike It's the wrong train.

Rodger About manifestation. Let's say you proclaim a thought. But there's a gap there, between the thought and the impulse?

Christen Yes?

Rodger What's in the gap?

Christen Nothing's in the gap.

Rodger You see, it takes a second for the electrons to move. There's a gap there, so there's time for change, there's time for movement. You're not even the same person anymore.

Mike But there's all kinds of organic stuff going on. The heart beats. The pulse. The liver. The guts.

Rodger But where am I?

Mike Oh, the hell with it.

Rodger Yeah.

Christen Shut up, Mike!

Mike The gap has no meaning.

Rodger Who says? You could say the gap has the only meaning, that between the impulse and the manifestation—what do you call that, the gap before the manifestation? You can call it God, you could call it the Devil. You could call it Nothing. And you can't get it back. You're there, you can't go back. And you threw her into the water. And you can't go back.

Christen Wait a minute.

Mike *We* threw her into the water.

Rodger No, sir. No way.

Mike Into the well. Who was she?

Christen We'll call her *Naomi.*

Mike She was fetching water in the desert.

Christen *We* threw her into the well.

Rodger And what is her nature now? And what was it then? *Naomi's?* And what will it be?

Christen We may never know.

Rodger There'll be another train coming, and I'd get on it, if I were you.

Mike She'll be gone by now, across the underground river and into the sea.

Rodger *C'est la.*

Christen What does that mean?

Rodger A *caesura.* The end of a thought. A pause.

Mike In the movies, she'd re-appear again, like a wet ghost.

Rodger What's to be done when everything's too late? It's written and done. Last page. Last dime.

Mike The Earth is not permanent, either.

Christen Who asked you?

Mike The Earth is not permanent.

Rodger Witches with premonitions and loaded dice. Never tell a woman she looks tired. Seaweed drifting off her like hair.

Christen This is a poem, really. Do you expect it to play?

Rodger I expect it to play.

Christen Like a roll of the dice.

Rodger Mallarme.

Mike I didn't follow that.

Rodger It's Fate. That which has already happened, but not formed into form.

Mike That fellow asks interesting questions. By what momentum does the storm blow? Is it an accident?

Rodger Maybe so.

Mike Meanwhile we blow the air around. Onstage. Ha.

Rodger Do we make a soul by falling down?

Christen No. By falling and struggling up again.

Rodger Agreed.

Christen No one wants to die. No one knows what it means. We threw her from the edge and she fell a long way. She'd be gone before she hit the water.

Rodger You threw her down the well and she drowned. *(Silence.)*

Mike Can you hear? *(Pause)*

Rodger Nothing.

Christen A body hitting water *(Splash)*

Rodger There is a well here, right in the center.

Mike It is a deep well, made of mortar and rocks and who knows what. The walls are four feet high above ground. Color: Gray. A bucket and a rope. We've all seen these wells, in paintings, in the movies, in the Bible. The desert well. The ancient well.

Rodger We haven't pushed her over yet.

Christen No!

Rodger I don't think so.

Mike Let's try again.

Rodger When I was a boy I could sense what was going to happen: endless, deepening suffering for which there was no cure. This is the same with this imaginary "Well" into which Naomi has yet to be pushed.

Mike I'm not following this.

Christen You never follow anything. You're like a donkey on a loop.

Mike What was that supposed to mean?

Christen We're talking about the inexpressible *Now*. That which cannot be said.

Rodger Wittgenstein.

Christen Right.

Rodger She leans over the wet wall and falls. She slips and falls. She loses her grip, first over the rope, and then the bucket. She falls. No sound.

Woman's Voice *(Off)* I'm falling! Help!

Rodger *Sound* of her body hitting the water.

Christen This is how the world ends. First with air and then with water. Gravity pulled her all the way down. She watched the stone walls go by without much interest.

Rodger *Sound* of her body hitting the water.

Mike At the bottom of the well.

Christen She has a thought and it's immediately gone.

Woman's Voice *(Off)* Help!

Christen *Silence.*

Rodger It's sand now. It's a desert. Fire grows in the cracks. Not life, *fire* growing in the cracks. The Earth is as hot as the Sun. The Earth is a satellite of the Sun.

Sol They had a schmuck for president and he lost the air and the water. That's one way to look at it.

Rodger Right.

Christen God, I wish he'd stop saying that.

Rodger He could not reason and the water evaporated and the atmosphere became carbon dioxide. Oxygen had already burned up the surface of the planet. That was pretty much it. We died where we were, gasping for breath. *(Another knocking at the door, insistent. Sol stands up. Christen cries uncontrollably.)*

THE END*

**It is very important that tension is maintained at the tables not speaking: all movement and behavior must be choreographed and set—this makes additional, but interesting, demands on the actors, and aids in the tension of the atmosphere. It is a play about the advent of tyranny.*

TWO VIOLINS

A MAN and a WOMAN onstage, both with violins. And a VOICE over, in italics.

Hey.

Yes.

A fig?

What?

You want a fig?

Ripe?

Yes.

Sweet?

Yes.

I'll try.

Good!

Amazing!

Try another.

Really.

There are thousands.

I know.

Right here on the tree.

Thank you.

You feel that?

What?

Your fingers.

What?

Touching my hand.

I don't know.

Try again.

Okay.

Try another.

Okay.

You feel that?

In my fingers?

Yes.

I think so.

What is that?

Electricity.

How is that?

It's our bodies. Good.

Oh.

We're electrical.

I see.

Our fingers touched.

Yes?

You feel that?

I think so.

What?

It's electricity. A spark.

Okay.

I know you felt it.

How do you know?

I was there.

Yeah.

It takes two.

Two?

Two electrical machines, like us.

I see.

It's a vibe.

I think I felt it.

I know you did.

What does it mean?

Polarity.

Oh. Polarity?

We're standing there, our bodies inching closer. And then we touched hands and there was a spark.

I didn't see a spark.

You felt it.

I don't know.

I did.

What did it mean?

It means there's an attraction. A current. Between our bodies. Between our fingertips. I thought you were going to grab my hand.

I wasn't.

It's rare, you know. To have.

What is?

That kind of electrical contact. It's rare. It doesn't happen much in a lifetime. Where you can say, you know, what a feeling. I'm not telling you anything mean. Our fingers touched.

Our fingers touched.

There was a tingling. And our bodies were moving toward each other. That must mean something.

What?

Electromagnetism. We're alive.

What to do?

Nothing to be done.

Do we live or die?

Now we live. Soon we die. Let's die. There was a shock of life, like touching a live wire.

When?

I was searching for bread. My father is lying on the street. My father is dying on the street. Some people walk around him, others walk on him, as though he were an old blanket. Trash.

We are walled in.

Yes. By the stupid and the ugly. Oh, how I would like to kill them all!

So, would I. The shithead local fire and police departments and all the lying sonsofbitches in the schools.

First things first. We need to find bread.

There are too many of us. And too many of them.

They are shooting a thousand a day, or so they say, *a thousand vermin gone today.*

Don't sing you idiot!

I'm sorry.

Don't rhyme!

I'm sorry.

We dug our ditches and then we take off our clothes and are glad to make the planet cleaner, free of Judaica, and we sing the *Shema*, and take a bullet, and our lives are over, completed by martyrdom.

What then?

What then?

What then?

Smoke, bugs, worms, what?

I don't know. We'll die and get it over with. We'll sing and die and play our violins, take a bullet in the head and then maybe we go to our ancestors.

Where is that?

(Pointing) Up there.

(Jumping) Here I come!

Not yet. Wait on the bullet in the back of the head.

No.

We'll find bread and not be dead.

We'll kill someone instead.

Who?

A Nazi. We'll grab him by the hair and snap his neck. And then we'll go on a spree. We'll kill them all.

Oh!

They have parties on the veranda while they watch us die. COME WATCH THE DYING JEWS AND HAVE A NICE MEAL. MUSIC AND DANCING! TWO VIOLINS!

Bread!

Veal sausage!

Wine!

Music!

Two violins!

That's us. And we don't have long. We'll give our lives for Mozart, Beethoven, and Brahms.

Ready to play?

Yes.

Unrehearsed!

Yes. Where's the audience?

They are there, behind the wall.

What wall?

Containing us, revealing us. Funneling us, you could say. Jewish blood going into the planet, it's got to help the planet. Like an infusion. Think of it that way. *(They raise their instruments as though to play, and a volley of gunshots is heard instead.)*

2.

You are mad. I thought you were mad before, talking about fingers and electricity, but now I'm sure of it.

You can think whatever you want. This is the End. A fig tree in the Ghetto, eaten to the bone. No, eaten to the bare idea of it. That's what we ate—the idea of FIG.

The Tree of Knowledge.

I don't think so.

Nobody knows what it means.

What?

The tree.

Somebody knows.

I don't know.

It means the End. Imagination, like the fig that wasn't a fig. A taste in the mind. An Essence.

Go forth, He said to Moses, bring enlightenment to the *Goyim!* What a joke that turned out to be.

The Hasidim in the East. They wouldn't fight. They kept to the Commandments. And almost the entire people were murdered. A remnant came to the U.S.A. in hopes of rectifying Jewish life in the seventeenth century.

No joke. You had Rabbis on the floor thanking God with their death rattles.

Why?

Because they had no chance at Life. And they wanted to stay kosher, so they said their prayers and gave it up. *Hear O Israel*!

The ones that survived, they came to Williamsburg and Monsey, New York.

Nobody gets in, nobody gets out.

And you have a man with Evil Intent over there and orange hair.

Where?

There!

Who's that?

I think he's over there.

Where?

There.

What the fuck?

Who is this person?

He looks like a mushroom.

He looks like a lightbulb.

He's electrified!

There's one, there, in the bushes. Don't look. If you look at him, he'll shoot you, as sure as night follows day.

I will not look.

He will not stay.

I could almost taste that fig you offered.

Was that him?

Yes, as our lonely fingers touched, among the corpses and the dying. I had a fig tree in my garden. I let anyone harvest them as they came by, Friday evening and Saturday in the morning and night, stopping to pick the fruit. A little prayer, a little fruit.

I'm an old woman in rags, bones and old flesh who can barely walk.

As time is passing.

The rest is dusty air, not enough oxygen, not enough light, dedicated to the death of all Jews everywhere. The Creators, really, of the Culture of the West. The Intelligence of the West. The Religions of the West.

It's too late now for Romance. That's your weakness, the big one, a pretty face, a girl's attention, the wink of an eye, those will get you any time.

You should make it the First Cause, from which all else flows.

Hail Spinoza and the First Cause!

No. The First Cause is the murderousness of the uncircumcised. Look how they do.

Shall we play?

Let's play. *(They start to play, but a series of loud antiaircraft fire goes off.)*

3.

Wrong cue?

You want to talk to somebody?

You'll go up to the ditch and take a bullet in the head.

No, you go.

No, thanks.

Who are they shooting at?

They should have bombed the camps. Long ago. The railroads and the barracks and the machine shops. The Americans and the British. They left the camps alone while the Germans carried out their butchery.

And so?

It's true.

And then they'd know we knew.

So what? Who cares? What could they have been thinking?

The anti-Jew in the home country.

Let's go. You and me.

You go.

No, you.

Let's take a moment to live.

Yes. I want to say yes. Take pleasure in what's left. The pleasures of the body. But all around they're dying or waiting to die, like you, like me. Like he or she.

Thing is, the harm is done now, the harm is permanent. Never to be undone.

Strange creatures. We eat and shit and blow air around. No wonder killing is such a thrill—

I'm not thrilled.

Just think—and Moses went forth, up on the top of the mountain and Yahweh spoke to Him from a cloud, Moses was not allowed to see Him, the Creator, only to listen and pass it on, this Egyptian boy found in the reeds along the Nile. And yet here we are, breathing the foul air of the Ghetto—watched by armed Ukrainian police.

I am not Ukrainian.

Does night follow day in this place?

Night follows day. The cosmic clock winds on no matter what we do, children of the One God.

I have not seen the Sun in many days. I don't know how many days; the days are vanishing. I no longer count the days.

You think you can kill that yellow-haired soldier?

No.

I am no longer a soldier.

What are you?

I am a messenger from the living dead.

He'll kill you first chance he gets.

How do you know?

Don't look at him.

Why not?

His eyes are red. Electrified.

Why do you say things like that?

Everything is electrified, down to the last breath. I saw you going by, a moment ago, and I was electrified; and I was mortified, as well, for once we could have been lovers. And now it's too late.

You remind me of the old times when men were students, and the women wore wigs. Now the wigs are gone, and the books are gone, and people are starving in the street.

What answers did they expect to find? In the books, in argument? What phrase or insight might appear to account for the mass murder of the messengers of God?

I'll have half the fig.

What are you afraid of? We are soon to die. On the ditch. A bullet in the back of the head. Just think. One thought. One last thought. Go ahead and think something, then eat the rest of the fig.

Thank you.

Keep you alive for a few minutes. Don't let him see you, the soldier in the bushes. Good.

Amazing what a look will do. A glance. I'm thinking of assassinating that stupid soldier.

How?

With our eyes.

Come on.

Half-closed eyes, and then you think—you want to direct the energy into his head. The electrified energy in the air. We concentrate. We think. We'll kill him with our thought. Think. *(A pause)*

I can't think. I don't have the energy to think.

Never mind. Can you play something Yiddish? Deedle-deedle-dum? That ought to do it.

No. Step away, you're breathing down my neck.

I'm not.

Step away. Let's play. *(They raise their instruments, but a catastrophic thunder of machine gun fire ensues.)*

4.

Well.

The music of gunfire.

People love that shit. Bombs, firecrackers, chases, and car crashes, shotguns.

Did he move?

I don't know.

I think he moved.

Not too loud.

Maybe a centimeter.

Can he see us?

Can we see him?

Definitely.

Then he sees us.

Don't look.

I'm not looking.

It might arouse his attention.

I'll turn away.

On second thought, he has no attention. Everything he has is on himself. Turn around, see if he moves.

I can't.

Try again.

I can't.

Are you welded to the stage, or not?

Not.

How could that happen?

Did the soldier move?

No.

Can you see his eyes?

No.

Don't panic.

Okay.

Don't try to move.

No.

I'm sorry.

Never mind. I don't think he sees anything when he looks. He has trouble looking. When he looks, he doesn't see.

What then?

He doesn't know what to make of it. He can't figure it out. His mother used to wipe his nose with an oil rag. And she wiped his ass with a wet dishcloth. He was a golfer man. He zoomed around the countryside with baskets of little balls and sailed with ease over bumps and thumps and wiped out everything in front of him.

Let's think about something else. Let's not think about him. Let's think about something else. Like the fig I gave you earlier.

I don't know what else to say about the fig.

The fig was from my garden, the Garden of Youth, where I grew artichokes and lemons, pomelos, and oranges. The world was fruitful then and I was too proud of my garden. And that's how we got down to one fig.

How so?

Pride. I had been blessed with an orchard. I did nothing to deserve it. And then a swarm of locusts ate the tree to its core. It was a dried-out fig, dry as paper. I used to skip my way to school and sing a jingle or whistle a tune. I had tangerines and tomatoes, chopped liver and prunes.

For lunch?

For lunch. *(Pause)*

Did he move?

I can't see him.

Don't move. Don't look.

I'm not moving or looking.

Sonofabitch could have a brain. Squeezed between his ears like apple sauce or drainage fluid.

He has a helmet on his head.

I'm standing here clutching my violin, frozen to the floor, and in the distance, I hear the crying of children. *(Distant sound)*

Don't listen.

Why not?

It's a tape.

You can't just keep on telling me things.

Why not?

Because I will revolt, I will recoil.

Okay.

And that will be bad news for you.

I'll take my chances.

I'll stomp your violin and cut your tongue out. *(Pause)*

Wait. Can I tell you about the tape?

Tell.

It was a tape.

You said that.

Children were gathering in the school basement and then the soldiers opened fire with anti-aircraft guns, flame throwers—and one of the idiots pressed *play* so all is recorded until the end of time. He was one of those guys who is sitting over there watching us for no fucking reason.

Maybe he wants to hear us play.

Let's play. *(They raise their instruments, and an enormous artillery barrage ensues. Pause.)*

5.

Not today.

No.

I remember you, in the old days, I remember you fondly.

What's my name?

I forget just now. But you had a wonderful body.

Yeah, yeah.

Absolutely perfect in every way. Blonde ponytail. Beautiful smile with good teeth, long legs, shapely breasts, a wonderful butt.

Did you try to call me once?

I did.

What happened?

I chickened out.

Try again sometime.

Yeah, like when?

Like tomorrow.

Or next week.

Or a year from now.

On the planet Mars or the moon. *(Forced laughter)*

I had tremendous yearning in those days. Too be fondled and fucked, hugged and kissed.

By me?

By you. Don't give up.

I'm an old man now.

Wait. I saw the soldier slink out of the corner of my eye.

Don't move, stay still.

He hates us.

That's how it goes. It's in the soil. They plant potatoes and up comes hatred of the Jews.

I'd like to kill the piece of shit, rip him apart with my bare hands.

Good luck with that.

Do something alluring. Get him to come over here.

No.

Why not?

He's *treyf*. Unclean.

How do you know?

That's a Nazi helmet he's wearing. Not a yarmulke. I saw him out of the corner of my eye. He might be dead. Look.

I can't.

Why not?

I can't get the right angle.

We'll never know, then. We'll be standing here stuck in the mud with eyes on earthquake and fire, flood, and hurricane. The History of Man as a planetary catastrophe.

I can't look at his eyes. They're red.

Red?

Red as blood. Streaming out of his head.

Don't tell me.

I'm telling you. Searing blood. Blood on the countryside, blood in the caverns, rivers of blood running into the earth. *(Sirens)*

I think he's made of cardboard.

No.

What then?

Steel. He's made of steel. Far as I can tell. Blood is streaming out of his eyes locked in on us.

Oh, come on.

Don't look.

He's a helmet on a stick.

Let's play something.

That won't work.

Why not.

The thing's got blood bazookas for eyes. Bazookas are the arms; fire is the armament.

Tell him to look away.

Maybe the music will hold him up.

He can't hear it.

Why?

He's got no ears. *(Pause)*

Let's go over there and hit him. Let's kick the shit out of him.

Okay. Ready?

No.

Careful with the instruments.

Yes. *(A rumbling sound)* What's that?

Sounds like an earthquake.

Sounds like whales. Sounds like singing whales.

Let's play. *(They prepare to play music but are overwhelmed by the loud onslaught of heavy artillery fire and whale song.)*

6.

Holy shit.

Let's wait a minute.

Let's sit down.

You got a rock to sit on?

I got a rock.

I got a rock, too. *(They sit)*

Well.

Well, well.

You know, I've had a crush on you for years.

Why didn't you call me?

I did call you.

So that was you?

Yeah.

Why did you hang up?

I chickened out.

Why?

I'm an elder.

So?

I didn't want to take advantage. And you're taller than me.

Too bad. Now we'll never know. The joys of sex, kissing and cuddling and excitement.

It's been many years now.

It shows.

What do you mean by that?

Nothing.

Come on.

You're still a good-looking guy, only now you have a big stomach.

It would get in the way of a good intercourse experience.

Oh, fuck.

Exactly. *(A few rocks roll onto the stage.)*

I have an idea.

What's that?

Let's throw rocks at the soldier.

He's nothing but a piece of shit. Armored.

Can you stand up?

Yes.

Remember, in the village square, we were standing cheek to cheek in the sun, thirsty and hungry, shitting and pissing in our pants. They had it blocked up with all kinds of shit like old trucks and cabinets and baby carriages, all four corners were blocked by the people who were having Champagne in the balconies above. And then a troop of killers marched in and set up a machine gun and opened fire. The square began filling with blood. There was a square of blood, higher and higher so we slipped and fell and after fifteen minutes the street was swirling with blood and bodies began stacking up on top of one another. I don't know who was in charge there. They were German soldiers and Polish and German gentlemen sipping Champagne and tea and eating little savories and I began to throw up and I ended up crawling under a building that had no foundation, there was maybe six inches of safety in there.

The blood in the square flowed down into the sewers and ditches and pipes into the earth, but the red square remained as it was to this day. Dried-blood red.

I made it back to the ghetto. People were dying on the streets. A perverted teenager wearing a Nazi helmet was going around shooting people in the head.

Was it him?

It was not I.

Was he a Jew?

I don't know. He was out of his mind, whoever he was. Don't throw rocks at that thing. *(Clang)* I think it's a piece of medieval armor, is what it is. Take care of your violin.

Right. So, Moses made his deal with Yahweh and they sacrificed the Golden Calf and then wandered in the desert for forty years. And thus began the History of the Jews and the pangs of Conscience on Earth.

What about Adam and Eve, Cain and Abel, Noah's Ark and Job?

It's the story of God. It was said to the Prophets, go forth and tell the *Goyim* about me and keep it simple and true—there is one God and he is Me and I am It. Turn your face away or the whole tribe will turn to dust.

He turned his face away. It was him. Him and the American Government. Millions could have been saved.

America was lame. They couldn't care less about the refugee Jews. Thousands had to go back and went to the camps and died there.

Shoveled into ovens.

Can you believe that? Can you conceive of that?

Let's kill the motherfucker.

Where is he?

Maybe that's him over there, The hulk. Blood coming out of his eyes.

He's a bunch of wire and light bulbs with a copper or aluminum shell. Throw another rock at him.

I'm holding a violin.

Okay don't throw it. This is fuckin' amazing. Tell the motherfucker to stand up.

Stand up motherfucker.

This area right here will no longer be an area.

Could you follow that?

What will it be?

Nothing.

I'm going to kill this sonofabitch.

Don't forget the violin.

No. Once we were mercenaries in the Arabian dunes. We rode camels and brandished swords. We lost a major battle to the Arabs. Imagine what could have been.

Soon you won't be able to breathe. We'll all drop dead where we are because the air is becoming carbonized and the oxygen is slowly disappearing, bubbling off the planet.

We know that.

Think of me as a mushroom or a fungus.

A mushroom *is* a fungus.

You get what I mean?

No.

Forget it.

You stupid motherfucking piece of shit. Trying to be a mushroom? It's gravity alone keeping us going, keeping us legit.

On the side of a wall.

Ask anyone what gravity is.

Hey!

Yeah?

What's gravity?

Why don't you go fuck yourself.?

Thank you.

Americans. Immune to the basics. Exceptional.

Let's go back to the romantic.

I don't feel like it.

We used to have lunch among the flowering plants and fruit trees and flowers. You remember that?

Yes.

What do you remember?

A feeling of subterfuge. Why? Because I had no rights at the time.

You were dreaming. You had no rights.

That's what I said.

You had the right to die. That's all.

Let me ask you—we got a sledgehammer around here?

We do.

Let me have it.

What are you going to do?

I'm going to knock this shithead into the ground, into the fire below. What do you say now?

I have nothing to say.

Here goes. *(A blow)*

Won't work.

Why not?

I am a permanent blemish on the History of Man. You can't chisel it off.

I'm tired anyway. I've shot my load. And there's been no love in my life for twenty-five years. *(Pause)*

We're so sorry.

No, you're not. I don't need no sorrows for me. I'm perfectly intact except for the hinges in my hips. Time was, I couldn't hit a nail with a hammer.

This is true.

Though you stood over me and abused me and bullied me.

Me?

Yeah.

Don't confuse me with someone else. I just wanted to get into your pants.

Well, you've missed your chance. No honey in the nest. But I made my own violin, which I will now play. It has a wonderful tone, borne of much suffering, worth about ten thousand dollars. In today's money.

(Starts to play and a huge avalanche is unleashed instead. Pause.)

7.

I have a theory of Everything.

Shoot.

All matter, all energy, all thought, all everything is a matter of refinement. And how is anything tangible or intangible refined?

Through suffering.

Correct. Hammering or burning, cutting, slashing, stabbing, pandemics, murder, what have you, it's all to make the course fine. And so, what have we done, we, the Jews, to carve out a piece of immortality, a fine substance in the heavens of a suffering martyrdom, a very fine vibration that wouldn't exist if it wasn't for us and the magnitude of our suffering.

Some people wouldn't go along with that. Some people said "Good Riddance."

The Universe wouldn't be the Universe if it wasn't for us. There'd be no music, there'd be no song, no clouds of burning light, of electrified matter. No burning bush.

Money. You all have money and a place to live, and you walk in a hurry like some Gentile kid might jump you and pull on your beard.

Where are you going? To and fro and in a hurry. And you stand and bow stand and bow, hours at a time. We are pounded mercilessly with Judgment of our sins, and we get down on our knees with remorse.

It's important to realize that there a chemical exchange going on. The Universe is a process.

This puts me in mind of my dear old mother. *(Pause)* She never caught a break. Beaten from the day she was born. Why? We don't know. Passed on from Ghetto to Ghetto, from Warsaw to Brooklyn, an unwavering persecution. From sewing machines to whacked with broom handles, to shock treatments to lobotomy, to advanced childhood at 85. There she was in Livingston Manor, in a home for the rest of her life, acting out at the age of six years old. We watched, my sister and I, as she cavorted happily about, playing with the other children, having lost the chance when she was herself a child.

They should have bombed the railroad tracks to the camps!

Too many Jew-haters in the U.S. of A. What was the name of that asshole, in the State Department, was it Long, a Mr. Long, who had the face of Death on him. American Death, superior white man death.

Bomb it once, and then a hundred thousand times!

Let's play something.

No.

Why not?

The crust of the Earth is loaded with bodies. Bulging with bodies.

Tune your instrument.

I am not a fiddler on the roof.

What are you?

Fertilizer. Look at this shit. Nobody will tell you what's up. They're too busy doing their thing, like watching TV, thinking about their teenage daughters, their wayward sons, their nasty wives, money, money, money and so on.

Meaning?

Don't kill me for this.

I had no intention.

Thanks a lot.

What are you asking?

I'm not asking.

What are you saying?

Don't tell anyone.

Why not?

It's a big secret. No one can know.

What?

We're all going to die.

Everyone knows that.

Yeah, but they are dreaming of immortality, heaven awaits these hypocritical American Christians. They believe all kinds of shit. While they shoot us in the back of the head and throw us into a ditch. Into the crust of the Earth. You get it now? We are imprisoned by Hate until the End of Days.

I do get it.

Buried in the soil is the shroud of the anti-Jew, buried there forever, waiting for his chance, and it's coming my friend, it's on its way.

Let's kill it.

You can't kill it. It's immortal. Maybe it was there at the beginning, as the planet was formed, like a chemical cloud or a cosmic ghost, there to squelch any rise of conscience on the face of the forming

Earth, there from the beginning, there until the end, knives drawn, cannon loaded, barbed wire—excuse me.

Why?

I'm going to throw up. And then I'm going to cry. And then I'm going on a killing spree.

Good luck. *(Pause)* What's holding you up?

It's like the head of snake or a giant worm. You cut off its head and right away it grows another one. What could that mean? We are abandoned, we are consigned to—

Murder.

What happened to Yahweh, he was supposedly our friend, we held him up come hell or high water. And now it's *Rosh Hashanah*, and we're supposed to rejoice and give thanks, and bow our heads to the Almighty and soon confess our sins and then to go on to live our lives under the shadow of Conscience, until they cut off our repentant heads and throw them into the endless fires signaling the end of the world.

Yikes.

You can watch the Holocaust on TV. Slivers of footage. The bodies of the dead and the soon to die.

Nothing will change. Life will go on and the memory will fade.

Say it isn't so, Joe.

Let's go to War.

Won't work.

Why not?

The people have frail brains in their heads, they can't get their heads around it. I don't know if I can. I'm sick to my stomach. I'm going to throw up again.

Watch where you're aiming.

I'm not aiming. I'm sick.

Okay, Joe.

Enough is enough.

Let's play. *(They start to play but are overwhelmed by a large volcanic earthquake eruption.)*

8.

Well.

Well, what?

That was a volcano. Probably split up a continent. Moved shit around.

Definitely.

What I want is to get to the bottom of this. Mainly in myself. Because nobody does anything or says anything or remembers anything and they love their silly jobs in dollar-land, so keep the borders closed because some battered hard-on walks in and shoots piss on our pigs. That's what they're thinking, like "Don't let those pimply ragged stupid black and brown faces in here, we have enough in this country, and we don't need you in here and that goes for the bearded Jews as well because they are not one of us, they are still living in the fifteenth century. I don't know where they came from or what they want from us."

They are coming from the death-camps.

Well, what is that? That's not our fault. That has nothing to do with us. We just want to make a living and we don't need people crawling in here or swimming the river or sneaking in on planes or the water ways. Or voting in our elections. And they murdered Jesus Christ, of all people.

When was this?

Fifteenth century.

That can't be true.

It's true.

Well, that's a big one. We got seventy million Christians locked up in the southern lands already. And that's not all.

What else? *(Pause)*

I forget now.

Jesus Christ, what a schmuck.

You guys got it all wrong. You are an idiot species of Man. The American bogie-head. You're not really men, you are more like pigs, and you piss and shit all over each other. So, what I'm going to do is this.

What?

I'm going to kill you all.

Why?

Revenge.

I got to go home now.

I got to feed the kids now.

I have an appointment.

There's a show I want to watch.

I'll be late for work.

I'll be late for my meeting.

I'm supposed to fuck my wife tonight.

I'm expecting a call from my dear old mother.

My father is in the hospital with contusions.

I have a date.

I never did nothing to nobody. Fuck that shit.

You don't belong here if you weren't born here.

They should stay in their own country.

We didn't have a country.

Fuck you then, we had nothing to do with your problems.

I take steroids for C.O.P.D.

I have diabetes. I need my insulin.

Anyone else? *(Heavy machine gun fire.)*

Fuck, man, we're all dead.

Like I said. I'm trying to figure this out. What do they have against us? Why do we have these gaunt white Christians denying our chances for survival? It's like these white heads are attached to the fungi. Talk about a worldwide conspiracy. It's everywhere on the globe, in the soil. So, I'm trying to understand it. In myself. I mean without the possibility of revenge. Of fighting back. Time moves on but something sticks. What is that? It is the remnant of conscience, because the species has a genetic error. Psychopaths emerge everywhere. One at a time, two at a time. In every generation. Black, brown, red, yellow, whatever. A psycho appears furtively. Even among the Jews.

While we play our lamentations.

Now it's something else again because the memory is fading and life on Earth is going up in flames.

So, it's a different ballgame. Our sorrow and revenge have nowhere to go. Not to the burning small-brained two-legged running for cover, not to the History of Man. And what of the evil spirit that aroused the European continent to murder its Jews. Why are we murdering Arabs? Will it remain in the atmosphere? Will there be an atmosphere? What remains—Like an amputation of the Spirit, even the idea of conscience, carved out by fire, flood, earthquake, migration, hurricane, and mass murder.

It's a song to the Universe itself.

Let's play.

Into the Nothingness above the Tree of Life.

END. MUSIC AND DANCING.

WHATEVER HAPPENED TO JULIE CHRISTIE?

A PLAY

Characters

Jethro	Retiring Academic, 70s; Chairman of Sociology Department. Memory and logic of associations lately becoming frayed. Uses a walking stick to get around.
Tyrone	Jethro's colleague and friend, not much younger; a Socialist Poet/intellectual.
Amanda	Tyrone's sexy 21-year-old daughter.
Betsy	Jethro's good-looking, androgynous, smart assistant; 35.
Constanza	Handsome, dark, Greek woman; in her late 20s.
Brad	Rich young American man who made his money in social media apps. A digital wizard.
Trent	An evangelical Christian youth.
Lady in a wheelchair	Heavy-set, dark, older looking, overbearing.

The Set

Brightly lit, shiny floor, with several chairs.

Speeches in *italics* are delivered Out, to the audience. Avoid entrances or exits. Scene breaks are indicated by asterisks.

Lights up and everyone is there, in place.

Tyrone What's going on, Jethro?

Jethro I had a bad dream last night. It was ominous and scary. You may remember, back in the day, there was a clutch of obese women in wheelchairs who were selling dope on the corner, near the old department. There was a little parking lot there where they hung out and sold drugs and the cops let them be for a while. You remember that?

Tyrone Yes.

Jethro It was heroin, Tyrone. You'd see them rolling in from all directions, and they had a loyal following—dope fiends and the handicapped and the mentally retarded. Finally, I had to get the city involved. Those crippled women were ruining the neighborhood. We couldn't have it. A flotilla of obese women in electric wheelchairs selling dope.

Tyrone I had a dream myself, Jethro. I was on another planet, staring down into a ditch. I was way up there. Down below was a man, a creature, staring back up at me. He had no face, but it was very expressive, very sad, staring up at me. The creature was all black and furry, with big white dots on him everywhere, and he was standing next to a perfectly wood-paneled ditch. *(Pause)* I don't sleep much anymore. It's like I want to get moving into the day.

Jethro Well, we've work to do, and time is running out. This is a task that will get you out there, Tyrone, break the solitude, and ease the embarrassed loneliness you suffer, daily.

Tyrone Don't tell me things, Jethro.

Jethro Someone with your background and size and shape. I don't know why I'm laughing. I know it's painful at times. I know the feelings—failure and isolation. Hurtling toward oblivion. We need the data: Is it as bad as we think? Where are we headed?

Tyrone We're headed for a breakdown, Jethro if history is a guide. Or, personally, a confinement somewhere hostile to our interests. I guess it will be good to have the data.

Jethro The first person I had in mind for you to interview is a young woman with whom I am acquainted.

Tyrone What's her name?

Jethro Her name is Constanza. A student of mine, Constanza Toomey.

Tyrone I will speak with her.

Jethro Good.

*

Constanza Are you following me?

Tyrone Yes.

Constanza What for?

Tyrone I'll tell you.

Constanza Tell.

Tyrone We're making a study.

Constanza Who is "we?"

Tyrone It's a University seminar. Dr. Jethro.

Constanza You're lying.

Tyrone No, I'm not.

Constanza I can tell by listening to you.

Tyrone Involution. The declining of faculties.

Constanza Whose?

Tyrone Ours. The Species.

Constanza Mass murder abounds.

Tyrone Yes.

Constanza Could happen anywhere, anytime.

Tyrone True.

Constanza For example, I hate men. No telling what I might do. Sometimes I think I have a tail. You expect to figure that one out?

Tyrone No.

Constanza Next one who bothers me, I'll cut his head off. No, I'll cut his prick off.

Tyrone I'm an Associate in the Social Studies Department.

Constanza Why me?

Tyrone You were highly recommended.

Constanza Oh. What for?

Tyrone Data.

Constanza Such as?

Tyrone What kind of music do you like?

Constanza Jazz.

Tyrone John Coltrane.

Constanza Yes. You might say in your report that some people are born happy, and then they stay happy for the rest of their lives.

Tyrone How so?

Constanza For no known reason.

Tyrone Are you one of those?

Constanza No. Some people are just happy. I'm a contemporary, hipster type of person. So, I keep a limit on white people.

Tyrone How?

Constanza I'm a migrant. It's easy.

Tyrone What kind of games do you like?

Constanza I like shooting galleries and cheerleaders. Shooting I like because you can tear a person apart with a gun. Cheerleaders I like because of the way they jump up and down and tumble around and shake their little butts and wag their stupid powdered faces and phony smiles covered with lipstick.

Tyrone Oh.

Constanza What you must do now is pay me.

Tyrone No. No money changes hands. Don't even think about it. You want to participate or not?

Constanza Not. You have a girlfriend?

Tyrone No.

Constanza What's her name?

Tyrone I'm single. A widower. Her name was Rose. She was a social worker. I have a daughter, Amanda.

Constanza My Grandmother and two aunts were social workers, here and in Greece. You know what "Auntie" means in Greek? Thea. Divine. In those days it really meant something. They visited people and took care of people. And they were political. On the Left. So am I. I don't care what you think. I want to get that out of the way. Capitalism is bad for Mankind.

Tyrone I tend to agree with you.

Constanza And so is the hatred of women and girls. It's all pervasive. It's in the yellow air we breathe. So, soon there'll be a war. Between us and you, between the women and the men.

Tyrone There'll be no one left on Earth.

Constanza There'll be a war, on Marxist principles, but organized by gender as well as class. It's on its way. Wait and see.

Tyrone If you say so.

Constanza I do. Something tells me you're a Greek, like me.

Tyrone Yes, Greek. I'm an Associate Professor, not a social worker. And I'm a communist, as well.

Constanza Good for you.

Tyrone Too late now.

Constanza Not to me it isn't.

Tyrone We missed the mark, historically.

Constanza I don't think so. People continue to lie and cheat. That's why I'm a Communist revolutionary. For real. White slaves don't matter.

Tyrone Excuse me?

Constanza Especially the boys. The girls have some taste at least.

Tyrone Where's this?

Constanza Right here.

Tyrone When?

Constanza Now.

Tyrone Sounds awful.

Constanza Pretty soon I'm going to buy a gun. And a sword. Watch out for fascism—it sneaks in there to protect the fat, rich, industrialist types. They bring in the heavy hitter racists and bankroll them. If I were you, I'd investigate that.

Tyrone I do investigate it.

Constanza You don't investigate hard enough. Your good days are over.

Tyrone Thank you.

Constanza Take my picture?

Tyrone No. Jethro thinks the cell phone is a disease. He doesn't believe in film. He thinks movies are ephemeral. And that they steal souls.

Constanza What's your name, sir?

Tyrone Tyrone.

Constanza What's the connection to the past, Tyrone? The real mimetic past?

Tyrone I give up.

Constanza The movies, Tyrone! The movies! *(Pause)* You seem stunned by that.

Tyrone Which movies?

Constanza That's it for me, pal. Move on.

*

Jethro She's a trip, isn't she, Constanza?

Tyrone She's dangerous.

Jethro There could be a screw loose there.

Tyrone A fervent communist.

Jethro Like you.

Tyrone More than me. And a moviegoer.

Jethro Have you seen an obese lady in an electrified wheelchair following you around?

Tyrone No.

Jethro You haven't seen her?

Tyrone No.

Jethro We used to have them clustering on the corner here years ago. They were dope dealers. Heavy-set women in wheelchairs selling dope.

Tyrone Right. You mentioned.

Jethro One of them wants revenge.

Tyrone How do you know?

Jethro It's the spirit of the thing. We were talking old age and death. We were talking about money. That's when you have problems. People rope burning tires onto you and throw you into the sea.

Tyrone Who's that, Jethro?

Jethro They were elected by the people. Why we sent you out there, Tyrone, to take the temperature. Listen to the people.

Tyrone Maybe it's the same as it always was.

Jethro Yes. People just plug in to other people's heads and repeat what they hear there.

Tyrone I'll tell you a great line, a masterful line, by Amos Oz, may he rest in peace. It goes like this, "What is it in me that makes me want to die right now?"

Jethro Quite right, Tyrone. You look into their eyes and—there's nobody in there. It's like they're waiting for Mad Max on the roads, raiding and roaming, hunter gatherers with trucks and motorcycles and armor. The only happiness is in the TV commercials. Everyone is smiling, everyone is having a good time. A heavenly America is in the commercials. So, everything's A OK. The citizens go on as though the myths of America are all true and operate somewhere in the sky. *(Betsy joins them.)*

Betsy It's the system, Tyrone, and we're on the verge.

Tyrone I'm aware of that.

Betsy Time for your meds, Jethro.

Jethro Thank you.

*

Betsy Keeping secrets, Tyrone?

Tyrone No.

Betsy There are hidden things.

Tyrone Definitely.

Betsy I feel like there's an aura of menace.

Tyrone Where?

Betsy Around.

Tyrone Whom have you met with so far?

Betsy I met with this guy, Brad.

Tyrone Yes?

Betsy He wants to take a chainsaw to the government. Tell Amanda to stay clear or I'll cut off her lips.

Tyrone A chainsaw?

Betsy Yes. It's an obsession. We will have to do assassinations, sooner or later. Like the Russians know all about this. They have poisons, you only must be in the vicinity and *boom*, you're gone. Or we get some aliens down here finally who can straighten it all out.

Tyrone We do what we do because we can't do anything else.

Betsy That's dark, Tyrone. I pray to my higher powers in the hope of salvation.

Tyrone Tell me more about Brad.

Betsy So, I drive out to meet this guy. Brad. He roams around wilderness areas and wants a companion. He's got a lot of money. He was formerly a digital tech person, whatever that is. It's too soon to know his thinking, if indeed he has any. Strikes me as a numbers guy. They pop up an algorithm and make a billion bucks.

Tyrone Capitalism triumphs.

Betsy I'll kill them all.

Tyrone Take it easy.

Betsy I don't know why I said that.

Tyrone Anything more about Brad?

Betsy He hasn't suffered enough. He's angry at the world. Especially the U.S. of A. He's a dork. Why a dork? The way he is—stiff and stupid. All he knows is numbers and algorithms. This is what happened.

Brad You must be Dr. Jones?

Betsy No, I'm not.

Brad How'd you find me?

Betsy I have higher powers.

Brad No, I made myself available.

Betsy Tad, the all-American boy.

Brad No. Brad.

Betsy Hello, Brad.

Brad If you're not Dr. Jones, then who are you?

Betsy Who is Dr. Jones?

Brad A therapist. He works with crazy people.

Betsy Got it. Let's get to work. You want to talk about politics or sex?

Brad If you're not him, where is he?

Betsy He's dead now, unfortunately.

Brad Oh.

Betsy Actually, he's a character in a book. Where have you been, Indonesia?

Brad No. Why Indonesia?

Betsy What do you want with Dr. Jones, who is not here and of whom I am not?

Brad Sex therapy.

Betsy I am not a therapist. And I don't like sex.

Brad What are you?

Betsy A social scientist.

Brad A socialist?

Betsy No. Are you always this stupid?

Brad I do think about sex all the time. And revenge.

Betsy Why don't you go get some?

Brad I live alone in wilderness areas.

Betsy I'm a pagan myself.

Brad Oh?

Betsy I believe in the stars.

Brad Nice. Come live with me. We'll make a plan. We'll topple the government and destroy the banks. I'm rich, and I think you're cute.

Betsy Forget it. I am a serious-minded person in need of social contact and intellectual stimulation.

Brad I contemplate revenge. But for you, I'll change my solitary ways. We'll work togetgher. We'll cut out all the fat.

Betsy Listen to this: "Dear Julie. And so, when I began to put myself together, so to speak, created my Platform, wired up my Data, and plugged in, my existence, my identity, was tuned to you, Julie. You were my model, my paradigm."

Brad Who is Julie?

Betsy Julie Christie. An actress. Try this: *Betsy goes into Jethro's office and sits down at his computer like she* *owns it. He follows, sighs with resignation, and sits across from her on the couch. He likes the office a certain way, so he knows where to find things. She ignores him and puts things anywhere. He can see her slim, little feet under the desk and stares at them for a moment, pretending objective interest to deflect her thinking that he wants to get into her pants. He's not always horny, but when she has a certain wistful look in her eye his sexual apparatus is suddenly activated, which stimulates his imagination. Her skin is smooth and white and silky and freckled. She could be the Princess of Norway. Full sensuous mouth that would make any old man think of magical blowjobs. Pink tongue. She beckons him over to look at one of her computer accomplishments and he bends over behind her so that his cheek brushes hers, so soft and downy and inviting.*

(A siren wails.)

"Reproduction," he thinks, a moment later, "on the Planet Earth."

Brad That was disgusting

Betsy You didn't hear it all.

Brad Where'd you get all that?

Betsy There are thought tapes. I just plug in.

Brad To what?

Betsy An outlet.

Brad Where are the outlets?

Betsy In the atmosphere.

Brad What was the siren?

Betsy That was the Thought Police.

Brad I see.

Betsy I could blow on you and you'd vaporize.

Brad Go ahead.

Betsy I'll save my breath.

Brad And the aliens?

Betsy Don't condescend. I could turn you into a wisp. They must come down special ladders, you know, and save us from ourselves and each other.

Brad Special ladders?

Betsy Special ladders.

Brad What are the ladders made of?

Betsy Light.

Brad I see.

Betsy No, you don't.

Brad I'm just saying—we'd want to be available. The best chance of that happening is in the woods, or on a mountain, or on the ocean with a missile-launching submarine.

Betsy The ocean is not the ocean anymore. It's a plastic garbage dump.

Brad If they're coming at all. I mean, the aliens.

Betsy You don't believe me?

Brad No.

Betsy Well, you don't know. You may never know.

Brad What do they look like?

Betsy What do you think? They're Spiritual Beings. Maybe you can't see them at all. They vibrate.

Brad They vibrate?

Betsy They vibrate. *Fast.* And they're blue.

Brad Blue?

Betsy Blue. You know who Plato was?

Brad Plato?

Betsy Plato.

Brad No.

Betsy Plato was a Greek philosopher. A forbear.

Brad Never heard of him.

Betsy I want to be ready when they come. Not the Greeks, the Aliens.

Brad I think the best thing is to stay out of the cities. I need a companion. I have a lot of money and no one to play with. You won't have to worry for the rest of your life.

Betsy Go back to the wilderness, Brad. Load up and practice your moves.

*

Betsy And then I'd about had it, Tyrone, I said goodbye, Pal, have a nice life. And then I ran into another guy who resembled him hanging around on the campus. His name was Trent.

Betsy Do you stalk?

Trent Stalk?

Betsy You know, *stalk.*

Trent No.

Betsy I'm afraid you're a stalker.

Trent I'm not.

Betsy I had a stalker. I told him I was through, and he wouldn't take no for an answer. He'd turn up in the oddest places. Across the street. Behind the aisles in the supermarket. Texts on the phone.

Trent Wasn't me.

Betsy It was someone who looked a lot like you. I tried to get a court order, but the police always showed up two hours late.

Trent What was his name?

Betsy Tad, or Todd. I told him I wouldn't fuck him, and he got weird. I don't fuck anybody.

Trent Too bad.

Betsy What kind of person are you anyway, Trent?

Trent Normal. If you think the world is going to hell, why don't you do something about it, instead of asking people questions?

Betsy I'm a social worker. I help people.

Trent There's no such thing as a social worker.

Betsy What about all those fires? The ocean is on fire. I hope it wasn't you that started all those fires.

Trent I don't start fires.

Betsy My survey question is this: Do you think we have like a new species?

Trent Possibly.

Betsy Say more.

Trent I think it's like being in a new species. Crawling around the earth in search of meaning.

Betsy I'm hoping for an intervention from above, myself.

Brad Stargazers. We lie all the time. This and that and let the Devil take the hindmost. Let's move on, Puritan. What do you do with your time?

Trent I travel around from place to place in search of meaning, in search of solace. Now I need a wife.

Betsy Not me, Pal. I have a job to do.

Trent Who do you work for?

Betsy Dr. Jethro is the head of the department. Jethro is a good guy. And he's an intelligent old hipster. But he's gradually losing his marbles and he can be dominated. He's starting to see things that aren't there. Soon he'll need refuge.

Trent You should come with me. We'll go places and meet new people.

Betsy I don't want to have anything to do with it. *(He makes a grab for her.)* Don't touch me!

Trent You have beautiful eyes.

Betsy Don't touch me. Don't call me. Don't text me. Don't stalk me. You do and I'll break both your arms. You got that?

Trent Yes. I do.

Betsy Good. Say goodbye.

Trent Goodbye.

Betsy *The survey is all a game to save Jethro from an Alzheimer's home. Or to put him into one and leave him there and forget about him. He can't figure out whether it's to save him or abandon him to the horrors of nothingness or, more than likely, the mere exercise of Ego and power on the part of his employees. In addition, he thinks, or he imagines a mad old woman in a mechanized wheelchair plotting and scheming to take away his rights. She seems vaguely familiar, a lot like one of his ex-girlfriends. He sees her occasionally racing up and down the garden paths of his L.A. condominium, an official briefcase* *in her lap, but he can't for the life of him remember her name, so he thinks he's dreaming. And maybe he is.*

*

Betsy You see the situation with this doofus—Brad?

Jethro I think I do, yes.

Betsy And Trent? They keep on texting me. And I've asked them not to. So, I'm going to call it quits. I'm going to put them both out of their misery.

Jethro That's entirely up to you.

Betsy Brad thinks the next world will be virtual, and the people will be robots. Or holograms. He thinks people won't have bodies. They'll just think their way around.

Jethro What about your aliens?

Betsy They'll have bodies. Blue. Hard to see in the sky on a good day.

Jethro I think of it as more of a moral/ethical question. Which means real people living bodily lives.

Betsy I know. But you see what's going on there? It's indifference and selfishness and who cares. It's the common attitude. You can't find a stand-up man anywhere. I can't. It's a desert out there.

Jethro I understand.

Betsy No, you don't. You don't believe me.

Jethro People do fall in love. It's a real phenomenon. Probably a genetic adaptation connected to—

Betsy The survival of the species.

Jethro Right.

Betsy There's a whole new kind of male person out there,

I can tell you that, Jethro, based on the interviews.

Jethro Give me more of an example.

Betsy The Army, the Air Force. Space people. Techies. The men who can tell you what's happening, but who won't say anything interesting. They play their seduction game with phones and computers and have no time for real romance, so they're a pain in the ass, and I won't fuck any of them. Even if I wanted to, which I don't.

Jethro I see. What about Brad?

Betsy Brad is a subspecies type of man who wanders around like a lost predator.

Jethro Trent?

Betsy Trent is the same or worse.

Jethro You can't get angry. You can't act superior. Even if you're good-looking, even if you're smart.

Betsy It's all so random. I wish the Aliens would come down and take me. Get me out of here. I don't like it here. There's no culture anymore. Only con-men and circus barkers and imbeciles. And techies. They're like robots, programmed to take advantage.

Jethro Let's talk about Brad.

Betsy I don't want to talk about Brad. Or Trent.

Jethro Forget it, then.

Betsy Brad. What a name. Brad. It sounds like cold shit.

Jethro Brad.

Betsy He's antisocial, maybe even a sociopath. That's what I think. Hanging out in the woods. A huge drag. A nerd psychopath. Calls himself a Christian. There's your new subspecies, possibly.

Jethro Maybe you'll give him another shot, find out about his political opinions.

Betsy He's a right-wing asshole. No question.

Jethro See him one more time. Confirm.

Betsy Then that's it?

Jethro Agreed.

Betsy I do know one thing.

Jethro What's that?

Betsy He hates dogs.

Jethro People who hate dogs are not necessarily right-wing psychopaths.

Betsy No, but they usually are.

Jethro Thank you, Betsy.

Betsy Why? I didn't give you anything.

Jethro *They're not up for it, the hard business of Life. Brain confusion. Leaves one in a permanent negative association. Like Betsy. I see no hope for it to change any time soon. "Fuck you if you don't like it." I'm glad to get to say it now, as I've seen the worst of the worst from what's supposed to be the best of the best: People with a mission. Personally, I have been completely (one could say deliberately) confused about my worth as a human being and the value of intelligence and talent. Revenge holds no way out, though I'd like to find one. Won't work. There's no self-knowledge, no sense of personal responsibility for anything by anyone. Like these girls have been saying. We need people in the streets. The youth. The young women. Armed, maybe. A restoration of justice and equality.*

*

Constanza What's wrong with you?

Jethro Nothing.

Constanza Don't blow in my ear, sir. Don't stand so close.

Jethro You know Betsy?

Constanza Yes.

Jethro She believes in aliens.

Constanza So what?

Jethro You have other things in common, like Communism. Revolution. Aberrant sex. Good things all.

Constanza I'm not a Communist. I'm a Social Democrat. She just doesn't like people.

Jethro She says there are Saviors from Above. On their way.

Constanza That's crazy.

Jethro Reports had it that you were a crazy person yourself, armed to the teeth.

Constanza I was gathering data on your boy, Tyrone, who was gathering data on me.

Jethro For example. You could be another species, for all I know, sneaked onto this planet after dark. No moon. No stars. Strange objects descending in a blue light...

Constanza Far as I'm concerned, I came out of my fuckin' mother and father, literally. Fuckin' sperms penetrating eggs. Quite primitive, really.

Jethro You curse a lot.

Constanza I'll tell you what they're thinking right now, the Owners, they're thinking we're crude and rude, and negative and hopeless, and should be shot. And one of these days, they'll open fire. I think we should all get ready to move.

Jethro And do what?

Constanza Organize. Build a fort or something. Print flyers, blow up bridges, fight like we're the Resistance.

Jethro The Resistance was a group of Jewish teenagers in Paris, lined up against a wall and machine gunned. The wall spattered with blood...

Constanza Okay. That's it then. I'll cope.

Jethro How do you cope?

Constanza I count. I count everything. How many times. How many boxes, how many squares, how many spirals. How many triangles. Nature is consistent and uniform. That's why I'm not an old-time Communist. It's pointless because we're rogue.

Jethro Rogue?

Constanza We don't fit in.

Jethro That's it for me, for the moment. I can't seem to find the next question.

Constanza The sun comes up; the sun goes down. Man stays the idiot he is. Nothing is learned. Just tearing each other's guts out. If not by gun, then by phone.

Jethro Thanks, Connie.

Constanza You're welcome.

Jethro I might want to talk to you again.

Constanza What for?

Jethro More of the same, I fear.

Constanza I'd come armed if I were you.

Jethro I think I will.

Constanza Bring your mind as well.

Jethro It comes with my head.

Constanza That's not where your mind is. Your mind is in your chest. It's called Heart. Bring your heart. You don't know much, do you? For an old sociologist?

Jethro No.

Constanza And you're going around taking a survey. How the degenerates are degenerating. I think that's awfully ironic. They'll be laughing at that one all the way home.

*

Tyrone Would you lie, Jethro?

Jethro Yes. Of course. We live with lies. Mainly it was genocide and a land grab and slavery what made the American economy. They plundered the resources, land, and sea, mountain, and prairie. Sacrificed the natives. Sugar and cotton. Black Man's Labor. Raise the alarm!

Tyrone No one will hear you, Jethro.

Jethro Poisoned water and bad food and snarky air and bombs falling on children.

Tyrone We're obsolete.

Jethro Cynical attitude, Tyrone

Tyrone Our students think we're dystopian.

Jethro We are.

Tyrone Speak for yourself. They want to put you away in a home. Or jail.

Jethro I won't let them.

Tyrone Make sure you have Power of Attorney.

Jethro I do. It's you.

Tyrone Not me.

Jethro Betsy.

Tyrone They'll find us under a parking lot in a thousand years. Charred bones. That's where they find people like us, prophets and schemers and twisted madmen.

Jethro Not you, Tyrone. You're an innocent. You died to yourself years ago. I watched it happen with my own two eyes.

Tyrone And you?

Jethro Someday I'll have to shut up because the mechanism won't work. I can't keep a straight thought, as it is. I think that sucks. And I thought you were a friend of mind. I said "mind." I meant "mine."

Tyrone Gotcha, Jethro.

Jethro So why don't you answer me?

Tyrone What was the question?

Jethro I don't remember now. Amanda will be showing up with a bunch of demands. She's going to want money and presents. She thinks it's all meant for her personal consumption. All the products in all the American stores. Here she is now.

Jethro I'm just an old hipster who's lost his way. I guess that was Amanda. Where is she?

Tyrone She was here a minute ago.

Jethro I missed her.

Tyrone Slippery little waif.

Jethro Stand in one place why don't you.

Amanda Betsy called me a thief, Jethro, and that's not right!

Tyrone Amanda?

Amanda Hi, Dad.

Tyrone Let's step aside for a second.

Amanda You want to hassle me about the future?

Tyrone No.

Amanda I want to work for Jethro as a steppingstone to higher things.

Tyrone Don't tease him.

Amanda I don't.

Tyrone He's a horny old man.

Jethro Are you talking about me? *(They move away.)*

Tyrone What higher things?

Amanda Eventually I'll run a restaurant.

Tyrone Seriously. I'm not going to be around forever.

Amanda Where are you going?

Tyrone I'm going for a walk.

Amanda Stick around, Dad.

Tyrone I want you to be safe.

Jethro Tyrone!

Tyrone Why are you yelling?

Jethro Why? Like Wild Klansmen cavorting on TV.

Tyrone Excuse me?

Amanda He's lost it, dad.

Jethro Make a report, Tyrone.

Tyrone Well, people are thinking all kinds of thoughts, like the Earth is flat and God loves the evangelicals and Jesus will save you, whatever you do, such as burning down prisons, thoughts like that.

Jethro Like a conspiracy? Are there meetings, committees, do they publish papers?

Tyrone We must move on, with more sophisticated data,

to another level. Wait. Here comes Brad for his second interview. Let's ask him. Brad?

Brad Quantum Theory. You know quantum?

Jethro No.

Tyrone No.

Brad The idea is two.

Jethro Two?

Brad Two versions of the same thing. In different spaces. Or side by side. Could lead to time travel.

Jethro We need to pursue a line of thought there.

Brad It's just a question of Time.

Jethro Ah! Listen to this tape I made for the future beings on Planet Earth.

Brad No.

Jethro Don't move. Pay attention.

America: The land of boobies and anti-Semites. Future Donald Trump Land. A liar, a thief, and a con. The chickens are coming home to roost. What to do? And the contradiction here is how much I still care. What is it all about? Must be natural to the species. We built a slave economy and killed off most of the native population and put the survivors on "reservations." They are there to this day. And the right-wing white guys are worried about the demographics. Does it mean a war? Could be. People don't reason or empathize, so it's likely, given the low level of the culture. The whites will try and kill off the coloreds. Likely attacks and bombings and massacres. Everybody thinks he's right.

Jethro What do you think?

Tyrone I think that's right.

Jethro Brad?

Brad The idea is to win. It's all in the numbers, digital and otherwise. But you got to win, you got to get there first. The internet opened all these possibilities.

Tyrone Do you read?

Brad Sure, I read. I read the Book of Nature. That's what I like. I stay out of the cities, anywhere too populated. Now I'm looking for Betsy.

Tyrone Why?

Brad The woman is strange. Something metallic about her, something pure.

Tyrone So why are you chasing after her?

Brad I can take care of her. I have money. We can have a nice time in the wilderness.

Tyrone She's not that type.

Brad She can learn.

Tyrone Professor Jethro here thinks the species has changed. The human species. He thinks there's a new organ in the human being, maybe, that is processing data.

Brad I think he's got a point there.

Jethro Yes! It has affected our intelligence and our morality. Somewhere on the planet right now somebody is getting their head chopped off.

Brad But the data stream is immense, streaming around the planet, an endless stream of electronics and information and imagery and thoughts and songs and God knows what, rolling around the planet like a ball of yarn. Or a skin.

Jethro Exactly right! It's another atmosphere or something, like the wind or the weather. Bands of Data swirling around the Earth.

Tyrone So, we've developed this organ to deal with it. According to Jethro. A new organ. A secret organ. An unknown organ.

Brad What is it?

Tyrone It's a Data Receptor.

Brad I think he's right.

Tyrone Or a lying acceptor. What do you think?

Brad Yes! A cloud of corruption, emanating from the very constitution itself. It's in the machines. That's why I like to stay away from society.

Tyrone Dr. Jethro doesn't think it's limited to machines. He thinks it's a sensory organ, or a gland, inside us, born into us. Or drummed into us.

Brad Where is it?

Tyrone We don't know. But we do use it to signal to one another through aggression and violence and the misunderstanding of simple things.

Brad Do you have one of those new organs?

Tyrone I probably don't have it. Do you?

Brad I probably have it.

Tyrone And then, there's the phones. What's their main intention, Brad?

Brad I don't know.

Tyrone Take a guess.

Brad To make money.

Tyrone No.

Brad What then?

Tyrone To bury conscience.

Brad And Dr. Jethro?

Tyrone It could go every which way. It's day to day. He sees all kinds of signs and omens and portents. We got three different pre-op programs for Jethro already up.

Brad On tape?

Tyrone Everything is on tape, Brad, even before it happens.

Brad That sounds correct to me.

Tyrone I just made that up, Brad. Ordinarily, I don't talk to people like you.

Brad Thanks.

Tyrone You're a twit.

Brad Thanks, again.

Tyrone Betsy tells me you're a Christian.

Brad No. Not me.

Tyrone Jethro thinks the worst has already happened. Not for the better, for the worst.

Brad I can't get into any of that.

Tyrone It's too much for anyone to think about.

Brad How much money you got?

Tyrone I don't need no money where I'm going. I do agree with Jethro. Old man on crutches, what's he going to do? What's he got to live for? *Me?* I'm thinking I'll take a pass and shoot up or take a walk in the woods.

Brad Dr. Jethro?

Jethro No joke. There's a species now, they can't go deeper, they can't reason, it's Darwin going backwards. I'll bet he never thought about that.

Tyrone He thought it was random enough.

Jethro No, he was some kind of optimist, taken in by the diversity and the beauty of English life. He wasn't thinking of the American Babbitt as Sinclair Lewis had it. Who remembers Sinclair Lewis anymore? Now it's all virtual reality and commercials. People like Brad here, without a social conscience.

Brad I just want to stay away from people.

Jethro I don't blame you.

Tyrone Jethro, do we have enough Data?

Jethro I think we do. But we'll continue. We won't stop now. Let's mix it up. Find the oddballs, the straight arrows, when we can, like we're doing, and then we'll graph it up and publish. When the time comes.

Brad What about the working class?

Tyrone They think alike. All the same.

Jethro Why we concentrate on the eccentrics and Bohemians, poets, and actors. Artists. Here's the thing: For every person, there's another one, just like him. It's like quantum. Types. Same vibe, two places, two bodies. They may look alike, or not, but they're the same.

Betsy *Truth is, Jethro knows nothing about quantum theory aside from the word, "quantum," and the huge significance of the word in his wobbly mind. It stands for the doubling effect of mediocrity and species decline. The same is true of the theory and practice of Romance. Aside from the occasional fantasy, Jethro's romantic life is over. Tyrone has pointed this out to him many times and, for the most part, Jethro is glad to be rid at last of the species obligation to woo and to bed.*

Jethro I don't know where I got that quantum idea. I don't believe in it. It could be Plato for all I know.

Tyrone Plato what?

Jethro I'm not sure why I said that.

Brad I'd like to see Betsy again.

Tyrone Sure, but she doesn't want to see you.

Jethro You're a special type, Brad, speaking of types. Conscience-free. When were you born?

Brad 1986.

Jethro You go to the movies?

Brad Occasionally.

Jethro You ever see *Dr. Zhivago*? It was made before you were born.

Brad No.

Jethro Julie Christie is in it. In those days, you know, they tried to make movies that had meaning, that had an aim of some kind besides making money—in this case, it was about the Russian Revolution, but it was really a romance, a romance about a fallen woman, Lara, played by Julie Christie. There was something about her that went right into my heart. It wasn't just her beauty—those clear blue eyes, that sensuous mouth—it was her poise, her dignity, her carriage, her walk. Her intelligence. I felt a yearning and a sorrow I haven't felt in years—that a human being such as she could live in this corrupt world with utter, absolute decency.

Brad I'm sorry.

Jethro No, you're not. See the movie.

Tyrone I'll get back to work now, Professor.

Jethro Good. Onward, Tyrone.

Jethro *I saw a lot of movies as a kid. I saw every picture coming through. Each reel got smaller and smaller as it rolled from theater to theater and the films got spliced at every single one. And I got a little jaded about the movies, which is true to this day—they hardly corresponded with my actual life. Obviously, as a medium, it never could, frozen in Time as it is. On the other hand, people model their behavior on what they see on screens. It's called mimesis.*

*

Betsy Trent?

Trent Yes.

Betsy My name is Betsy.

Trent Are you following me?

Betsy Yes.

Trent What for?

Betsy I want to get to know you.

Trent Why?

Betsy I want to know how you think.

Trent Why?

Betsy It's an assignment.

Trent From whom?

Betsy My teacher. His name is Jethro.

Trent Well, goodbye and good luck.

Betsy I'm not going.

Trent I think you should go.

Betsy No.

Trent I'll call the police.

Betsy Call.

Trent Okay, what do you want?

Betsy Just to talk.

Trent Talk.

Betsy How do you think?

Trent I don't think.

Betsy You don't think?

Trent No.

Betsy What do you do?

Trent I react.

Betsy You react?

Trent Yes. I have feelings.

Betsy Such as?

Trent I like people and I hate people.

Betsy Both?

Trent Yeah.

Betsy How so?

Trent I hate people who think they're superior. I like people on my own level.

Betsy And me?

Trent I don't know yet.

Betsy How do you know when you know?

Trent That's a dumb question.

Betsy Don't answer it.

Trent It's a feeling.

Betsy I like people who are not afraid to lie.

Trent I'm not afraid to lie.

Betsy Tell me more.

Trent You'll have to pay me if you want more.

Betsy No. We have no money. We're a social studies program.

Trent Not another word.

Betsy Come on. I'll make sure you are mentioned by name and get a lot of credit for honesty and sincerity.

Trent I'll say one more thing.

Betsy Great.

Trent Free.

Betsy Shoot.

Trent I like people who love themselves and don't try to hide it.

Betsy Why?

Trent I don't know why.

Betsy You must know a little why.

Trent They make me feel safe. And at my level or slightly above.

Betsy Makes perfect sense.

Trent I think so.

Betsy Anything more to say?

Trent They respect my status and care about my income.

Betsy How do they know your income?

Trent I don't know how they know. Or, I know, but I won't say. That is to say—the banks. People know. They look at your standard of living, and they know.

Betsy Should everyone have the same income?

Trent No. That's Communism. Some people are better or smarter than others and should have a higher income.

Betsy Who are they?

Trent People who run the country, and make products, and that's all I'll say.

Betsy What else, Trent? Remember, you're being recorded for posterity.

Trent White people should have more than Black people.

Betsy Why?

Trent They're still tribal.

Betsy The Whites or the Blacks?

Trent The Blacks. And that's all I'll say. Except the Jews should go back where they came from.

Betsy Where did they come from?

Trent That's it. Nobody knows. They're aliens.

Betsy They're aliens?

Trent They're aliens.

Betsy Sounds like they're my kind of people. I must have some of that Jewish blood. Why should anyone, like the White people, have more money than you, for example?

Trent Because they take care of me and have my interests at heart.

Betsy Good, Trent. I'll make sure the right people hear about this.

Trent I'll tell you one more thing, because you look harmless to me, a harmless female.

Betsy Tell, Trent.

Trent The second coming. It's arriving soon. You can hear the rumblings from the East. We evangelicals are preparing the way. First the Jews must be defeated and scattered, and then the Christ will be here on Earth again. And those of us who are pure will rupture up to Heaven. I mean *rapture*. Up to heaven.

Betsy You jerk. Trent? I'd like to chop your stupid head off.

Trent Try it.

Betsy Never mind. I'll just think you away in a few minutes. Less energy. By the way?

Trent Yeah?

Betsy You look just like Brad. Is there a reason for that?

Trent I don't know no Brad.

Betsy Look in the mirror sometime. You'll see Brad. If Brad looks in the mirror, he'll see Trent. Weird. You're toast, Trent. Your cue, Tyrone.

Tyrone *"Marching, Marching's the thing. We don't have enough of that. We need to be in the streets. Don't break windows or start fires—march. March through the barricades. March for the right to be decent people against all odds. March over the police and the army and the galactic robots. March! What happened to the marchers, the heroes of the Left, the bearers of conscience? Where are they? Where have they gone?"*

Constanza We have a new class of people. A new primate type: Masters of the universe stuck up the Junk hole.

Jethro That's overstating it, Connie.

Constanza I was never impartial. I was depressed, but not impartial. My ego is a monster from the deep. Why? Because I felt superior to my parents.

Jethro Tyrone?

Tyrone Yes?

Jethro They'll be coming for me, as in the days of old. It's the wheelchair lady. Knocking on the door. Banging on the door. You hear?

Tyrone No.

Jethro Take your wife and kids and flee to the country.

Tyrone I have no wife and kids. Just Amanda. Amanda is all I have.

Jethro Sorry.

Constanza I did hear of a lady in a wheelchair hanging around.

Jethro For what?

Constanza She claims you have done her personal harm.

Jethro And?

Constanza She's out to get you back.

Jethro Where did you hear about her?

Constanza At a meeting.

Jethro What kind of meeting?

Constanza School.

Jethro School?

Constanza School.

Jethro Our school?

Constanza Yes. Last days.

Jethro What does she look like?

Constanza Normal, except for the wheelchair. She's overweight. Also, I think there's a loose pebble in there. A scruple.

Jethro Find out her name. Get her data. And I'll tell you why. She's been in my dreams lately. Either that, or I've seen her sneaking around. An obese lady in a wheelchair, stacked with dope and armed to the teeth. Don't tell me anymore.

Tyrone You still want to know her name?

Jethro No. I know her name. *FATE*. It's just Fate. *Nemesis*. The Greeks knew, so you should know.

Constanza People don't realize the danger. They don't see what's happening. It'd all be just another event. No one sounds the alarm. All the news is happy/neutral. No change of tone. Never mind. I was just guessing at your thoughts. Boring. Books to read. Tests to take. Bullies to kill. So, bye, bye.

*

Amanda What would you say is wrong with you, Jethro?

Jethro Someone else asked me that recently.

Amanda Who was it?

Jethro I think it was your father, Tyrone.

Amanda He should know.

Jethro He does know.

Tyrone We all have problems.

Amanda What's wrong, Dad?

Tyrone I feel like an idiot.

Amanda You're not an idiot.

Tyrone I am an idiot. Students sitting there leering at me, mocking me.

Amanda What happened?

Tyrone I telephoned your mother. A student of ours, Constanza, knew somebody who knew somebody who had her number. I don't know what came over me. I was delighted. I didn't pause to think it over, and I called.

Lady Who is this?

Tyrone Tyrone.

Lady You're kidding.

Tyrone No, it's me.

Lady Fifty years later and you call me?

Tyrone How are you?

Lady I can't talk.

Tyrone Why not?

Lady I'm a tired old woman and my brother is dying.

Tyrone Amanda is around here somewhere.

Lady Hang up. Don't call me. It's absurd. I don't want to hear your voice. Goodbye.

Tyrone Wait! It's confirmation, or validation, that we were married once in the real world. And have a daughter.

Lady Give my love.

Tyrone I will.

Lady Take a hike, Tyrone. Vanish quietly. *(Pause)*

Amanda I'm sorry, Dad.

Tyrone We went to Oaxaca together for the Party. We went to Mississippi for SNICC. We went to rallies and demonstrations and stood up to the cops and the rednecks and the hard hats. And now? All gone.

Amanda Do I look like my mother?

Tyrone Yes.

Amanda Don't cry, Dad.

*

Amanda So, Jethro. Betsy is ripping you off every chance she gets.

Jethro How do you know?

Amanda She has a thief's nature. She likes grabbing things. Like CDs and books. Am I right?

Jethro You fuck around too much.

Amanda I'm a virgin, Jethro.

Jethro Of course.

Amanda You ought to know.

Jethro Born in an egg, die like a piece of paper.

Amanda I'm afraid you're deluded.

Jethro So what?

Amanda Imagine the exchange of all those sticky bodily fluids.

Jethro So?

Amanda I meant to say that earlier.

Jethro A thousand bucks.

Amanda No.

Jethro Then I'll go into permanent exile. The mysterious disappearance of an eminent old academic—

Amanda —Died with his pants on.

Constanza *(Nearby)* May I interrupt?

Jethro No.

Amanda Tell Betsy to chill. I don't want the job anymore.

Jethro No?

Amanda You're paranoid, among other things.

Jethro What other things?

Amanda Deluded, like I meant to say earlier.

Jethro You did say it.

Amanda I'm done then.

Jethro Have a heart.

Amanda No.

Constanza I'm going to plot a revolution. Join me. It'll start with a mass killing of white males. Move on from there to fat women in wheelchairs. And snotty teenage girls.

Amanda Include me out.

ACT TWO

Jethro *So, God took a molecule and cut it in half and that's how we got two sexes, as the molecule divided and multiplied and we live through the inevitable joys and terrors caused by the situation, the sufferings of completion and loss, rancor and regret, happiness, and sorrow, and so on and so* *on. Race got in here somewhere along the lines of history and geography and sheer accident. We will not see the end of it in my time, for sure, and not in your time, either. As far as the Jews are concerned, hatred of and the blaming of the Jews has become as much a part of the planet as lava moving up through the cracks and volcanos exploding—hot and endless—a part of the meaning of the Earth. The Planet Earth, a blue rock covered with oceans circling the Sun. The Ontology of Mankind. The irony, of course, is that the mission of the Jews, according to God's instructions to Abraham, was to civilize the two-legged pagans of the planet and teach them the ways of the Almighty.*

Tyrone Let's run the data, Jethro.

Jethro No. Not yet. Let's get through this guy Trent. Have you seen Amanda?

Tyrone No.

Jethro She was just here.

Tyrone She's taking a pause.

Jethro Why?

Tyrone I don't know why.

Jethro Okay. Trent.

Tyrone He's coming over.

Jethro Here he comes.

Tyrone You talk to him.

Jethro I don't know the guy.

Tyrone Get to know him. Trent?

Trent Yeah?

Jethro You seen Amanda?

Trent No.

Jethro She was here a minute ago.

Trent I haven't seen her.

Jethro You seem troubled.

Trent I'm not troubled.

Tyrone What's the problem, Trent?

Trent Jews will not replace us.

Tyrone I don't get it.

Jethro Who wants to replace you? You are perfect automatons as it is.

Trent I'll say it again: Jews will not replace us.

Tyrone What is that supposed to mean?

Trent What it says.

Tyrone I still don't get it.

Jethro I'm a Jew, Travis, and I wouldn't mind killing you right now. With this club. *(A walking stick he keeps by him.)*

Tyrone Hang on, Jethro.

Jethro No.

Trent They think they're better than us.

Tyrone Who? Me?

Trent No. The Jews. Like him.

Jethro Maybe we *are* better than you. Get your head together, Travis.

Trent Trent.

Jethro Or your life's in danger.

Trent I said my say and that's it and that's all.

Jethro Drop it, dope-head, and I'll tell you something about humanity. There's smart ones and dumb ones. The dumb ones resent the smart ones because the smart ones make all the money.

Trent I don't know if I followed that.

Jethro And then there's culture, Trent, of which you have none.

Trent We have a Christian culture, Jesus-oriented. It's a new American battle cry.

Tyrone Nonsense.

Jethro My friend, Tyrone.

Tyrone We've met.

Jethro He's a Greek Communist.

Trent No excuse.

Tyrone It's barbaric, this so-called religion of yours.

Jethro Not the way to go, Tyrone.

Trent We're tired of the Jews.

Tyrone The guy on the wall over there is a Jew.

Trent Where?

Tyrone *(Pointing)* Right there.

Jethro What's your problem, Trent?

Trent I don't have no problems.

Tyrone Nothing personal.

Jethro Just a data point is all.

Trent We can do our own civilization—white and pure.

Tyrone Good luck with that, Travis.

Trent Trent. We got you people figured out, Mr. Jethro. You go back to the Neanderthals.

Jethro Yikes.

Trent Yeah, and you're one of them, too, Tyrone.

Tyrone I'm an atheist. Greek. Rational.

Trent What do you believe?

Tyrone I believe in nothing.

Trent Nobody believes in nothing.

Tyrone Except Communist ideals.

Trent Ha! The true whites of the land will find you out.

Tyrone And then what?

Trent We'll take serious action. We'll take measures.

Jethro Let's kill this hater right now.

Tyrone Not worth it.

Jethro You're excused, Mr. Trent.

Tyrone You look just like Brad.

Trent You must mean, Tad.

Tyrone No, I mean Brad.

Trent I don't know no Brad.

Tyrone Maybe it's Travis, then.

Trent I don't know no Travis.

Jethro Never mind. Go over there, Trent. *(Trent moves away to another chair.)*

Tyrone I'm scared, Jethro.

Jethro You should be.

Tyrone Maybe we drop the inquiry and run for the hills.

Jethro One or two more interviews.

Tyrone Why?

Jethro Data.

Tyrone I can't do it anymore.

Jethro Why not?

Tyrone I can't act innocent. I'm cynical and corrupt. Like the country.

Jethro No, you're not.

Tyrone And I'm tired and shaken. This person Trent is a menace.

Jethro One more.

Tyrone And then, that's it. I'm done.

Jethro Take a break, Ty. I'll handle it from here. *(Tyrone moves* *away.)* Come back here, Trent. *(Trent returns.)* I'm not through with you, Trent.

Trent Who cares?

Jethro It's a good thing we have police and an army. So that order is kept, and justice is done.

Trent That's a joke.

Jethro And public schools thrive, and garbage collectors make a living wage.

Trent The Government is not legitimate. They hire Blacks and Chinks and Mexicans and Arabs who don't even belong here. And the Jews run the whole thing plus the media. I'm not giving any of my money to support that. And it's the Mafia that controls garbage collection. Guineas and Jews. An unholy alliance.

Jethro I'm going to turn you in, Trent.

Trent Go ahead.

Jethro I'm going to have you arrested.

Trent This country should be all white and everybody who works for the Government should be white.

Jethro I'm a Jew, but I don't do anything Jewish. I was born a Jew and I identify with it and feel superior about it. Where would the world be without the Jews? Think it over. And I wear a Star of David, as Above, so Below, and have revenge fantasies about the Germans. Otherwise, I live the academic, secular life.

Trent Good for you.

Jethro And I'm about to retire. So. To continue: What's your personal history?

Trent I'm an all-American kid, I played ball and obeyed my parents and listened to my all-white teachers and went to church and hated the minorities and the immigrants coming over to steal our jobs our money and our women.

Jethro Okay. Thank you. Tell me more about your parents, Travis, if you don't mind.

Trent Trent. They're white.

Jethro I don't mean that—tell me about their brains.

Trent Are you implying that they're stupid, or what?

Jethro I'm saying that they may be an adaptation. An adaptation to the changing conditions of life. The environment.

Trent I don't get it.

Jethro Mutants, Travis.

Trent Mutants? That's outrageous! Come over to Idaho sometime, pal. I'll show you some mutants you won't believe!

Jethro I think I'll stay right here in L.A.

Trent Well, don't make any plans. Because L.A. won't be here much longer.

Jethro Where will it be?

Trent It'll fly off into space, like a burning movie. Take my word for it.

Jethro A burning movie?

Trent I don't know where that came from. Wow.

Jethro Still waiting for Amanda, Trent?

Trent Yes, I am.

Jethro Why?

Trent The movement of the stars. A congruence of celestial bodies. The music of the spheres.

Jethro How clever. Tyrone?

Tyrone *Reminds me of the time, down in Macomb, Mississippi.*

I was starting to crack up from the anxiety and tension—so I decided to make a little escape for a few hours and followed a narrow path on the Manning place which led deep into the woods. After a while, I began to hear music. The music was nothing like I'd ever heard—not in East New York or Downtown, or Harlem, or anywhere. And I'd been in some heavy–hitting Black Gospel churches. This music was celestial and got louder as I followed the path. Not only was this place hidden in the woods, but it was also somehow powered up by a secret cable connection to an outlet or a pole somewhere. The place was an electrified barn, and everyone was jumping to the vibe, the musicians and congregation joyously dancing and singing—no whites were there but me as I crept closer, and no inhibitions whatsoever. There were guitars of every kind, all electrified, horns, drums, tambourines, flutes, all on the same wild, happy page. And a preacher on the mic singing at the top of his lungs. My heart was pounding, and I thought I should leave them to their private holy celebration, but a dancing old lady saw me and waved me into the back of the room, where I stayed until dark, when it was time to return to the Manning House. They were still going strong in the barn when I left. God willing, I'll never forget that joyous afternoon. In the barn. In the Mississippi woods.

Jethro Thank you, Tyrone.

Trent That was painful.

Tyrone Oh, fuck off, Trent.

Jethro Here's Amanda.

Amanda Why are you standing there, Travis?

Trent I have rights.

Amanda We have the data, so you can go home now.

Trent I'm in love with you.

Amanda How strange. We've never met. And I'm a virgin and I plan to stay that way.

Trent I'm a virgin too.

Amanda How nice for you. But I don't entangle with anti-Semites. So, forget it.

Trent You're not Jewish.

Amanda I'm Jewish in spirit.

Jethro Amanda!

Amanda Take a hike, Travis, my boss is calling me. Bye, bye.

Trent You'd best disentangle from the Jews, Amanda, they'll drag you down into hell. I'm trying to warn you. The end times are coming, and you will be left down here to drown in a ditch. *(Amanda picks up Jethro's walking stick.)*

Amanda You see this club, Travis?

Trent I see it.

Amanda I'm going to bludgeon you with it now, you dumb racist sonofabitch, and then I'll bury you in a dung-infested ditch, maggots and all.

Trent Don't hit me!

Jethro He'll burst like a poisonous insect.

Amanda Get out of my sight! *(Trent ducks away.)* Answer me, Jethro.

Jethro What are you asking me?

Amanda I want you to fire Betsy.

Jethro I thought you refused the job.

Amanda Get rid of her.

Jethro Why would I do that?

Amanda She's taking advantage.

Jethro How?

Amanda Flirtation and dissertation.

Jethro That's the wrong usage of the word—you mean desertification—but go on.

Amanda She's been diddling you and dissing me. Is that what you want?

Jethro No.

Amanda I'm not trying to be hard on you.

Jethro Yes, you are.

Amanda No, I'm not. As my father has been trying to tell you: You will never, ever get laid again.

Jethro Thanks a lot, but this woman, Betsy, is androgynous. She has no interest in sex whatever. So, I have other plans. I defy you all. I still have dreams. I still have imagination. Something awakes in me, like a Japanese lizard monster. Women enjoying sex. Makes me wistful and insecure. *(Pause)* Do you find any of this interesting?

Amanda No.

Jethro I been meaning to tell you a story. A morality tale.

Amanda Oh, no.

Jethro It's your father's. Tyrone?

Tyrone Well, I was living on the Lower East Side in a two-room slum. Bathtub in the kitchen. I was still a virgin when I was nineteen. I never knew she had a crush on me.

Karen. I was a good-looking guy then. One day she looked me up in the city and we made love for two days. I was too insecure to make anything out of it.

Amanda Another of your many romantic regrets.

Tyrone Yes. A year goes by, and she comes again to tell me there'd been a child. I feel bad about it to this day.

Jethro Your father's too radical by a country mile.

Amanda So am I.

Tyrone Listen. Sex, the act of reproduction, can be stoked by fraud and delusion and deception.

Amanda I've heard all this before, Dad.

Tyrone And bad outcomes.

Amanda Yes. Like people born with four arms and five eyes. And it's us, America, leading the way. Look at the TV commercials and the cheerleaders. It's frightening.

Tyrone It is.

Amanda There's no right and wrongs no more.

Tyrone No.

Amanda What was I expecting? What was I thinking? Disgusting American Capitalism. Sorry. Not your fault. What am I trying to say? They take advantage.

Tyrone I know.

Amanda So, I worry.

Tyrone Don't worry.

Amanda I worry about you.

Tyrone I can't change now. It's too late now.

Amanda They take advantage.

Tyrone You said that.

Amanda Fire Betsy.

Tyrone It's not up to me. You do, too, you know. Take advantage. Like games with Jethro. Taunting and incitement. Titillation. Yes, or no?

Amanda Yes.

Tyrone Seedy of you.

Amanda Sorry, Dad.

Tyrone Somehow, it's all my fault. I spoiled you. I never said "No."

Amanda I understand what Betsy gives you guys. Charm and youth and company. What does she get in return? Money. Yes. It's a transaction, like everything else.

Tyrone I don't pay her. Jethro does.

Amanda She's got your number, Dad.

Tyrone Oh?

Amanda Femininity, drugs, hard rock and old-timey jazz...

Tyrone Those days are long gone.

Amanda Yeah, but you like the vibe. She gives you the vibe, metallic though it is.

Tyrone Occasionally. The libido fades. And she's asexual.

Amanda You're still susceptible to her feminine charms.

Tyrone Yes, I am.

Amanda Jethro flirts with me now.

Tyrone He doesn't mean it.

Amanda The nicest girl with the nicest background, she goes away to the city and two years later she's a whore.

Tyrone You watch too much television. Don't do anything stupid.

Constanza I thought I saw the wheelchair lady sneaking out of the building. She seems to think that certain crimes have been committed.

*

Jethro *Apropos, an old nemesis of mine comes around and I realize I can't stand her because I can't stand myself. Just a stupid emotional habit, which I'm getting rid of at last. No more of that self-put down stuff that happens by itself, automatically. But I'm starting to catch it now, at the source, which has continued to reshape my self-image, which is mainly nothing. Like the stupendous ego, arisen in childhood. There's these four or five topics I constantly ruminate over. That's about it. Same five topics, over and over.*

Constanza I heard again from the Lady in the Wheelchair.

Jethro Oh? What else did she have to say?

Constanza It was voice mail: "No more. No more fantasizing, no more wooing, no more sex." What's that all about?

Jethro We'd had an affair, back in the day, when she was still whole at the time.

Constanza Really?

Jethro No. I just made that up. Sorry. There was a tribe of them, buying and selling dope. I called the cops.

Constanza Turns out she wants you to drown yourself in a *mikva* or retire to a rest home.

Jethro Oh.

Constanza What's a *mikva*?

Jethro It's a ritual bath. I didn't want to be hurt. All those little cuts. When I knew the Lady, she offered sex, and I took it. Then she thought she owned me.

Constanza Makes perfect sense.

Jethro I was young at the time.

Constanza You just made that up, Jethro. That's okay. Dream on. Nature rules. Nature decides. Take note: War is bubbling up out of the culture, the politics. You can build a thousand-mile wall and Nature will flick it with her little finger into the darkness of space. You can hide in a deep hole, and she'll dig you out with an earthquake and hang you from a whanging telephone pole.

Jethro Thank you.

Constanza You got to watch out because people don't necessarily know what they're doing. They can think they're saints or great warriors and they're just little shitballs running around and getting in your ears.

Jethro What are you up to, Connie?

Constanza I might do anything, like shoot up a bunch of working cheerleaders at a Texas high school Friday night football game. Stay tuned.

*

Jethro And suddenly, I'm losing my temper and yelling things. I'm yelling things, and limping along with a cane, and wearing a fedora—elderly Academic, hobbling along.

Tyrone At least we're not chasing after people and compiling data on them, which is the last thing I want to be doing.

Jethro They're planning it now, Tyrone. The right-wing thug heads and fatheads are drawing plans onto paper bags. As we speak. Paper bags and paper towels and napkins and notebooks and pamphlets, and other war-like actions.

Tyrone Actions?

Jethro Yes. How about armed insurrection?

Tyrone Seems unlikely.

Jethro Connie Toomey was just here. She likes you.

Tyrone That's nice.

Jethro And what do you recall about the Lady in the Wheelchair?

Tyrone We turned on her in one fine winter's day. Years ago. Remember? They put her in an ambulance. It was snowing. She struggled mightily, like a force of nature. Now, vengefully, she wants to confine us to a rest home or some other facility for the old and infirm. Or die.

Jethro *Nemesis*, like I told you.

Tyrone After that my ex inserted me into a rehab facility in Malibu. They invited me to stay, and I stayed, despite the contradictory data. They told me I wasn't an alcoholic but was certainly medicating myself. They took the money of course. I lived a different life in rehab. The wise old man on the hill. Alone. All my friends were no longer my friends. Not a single person called. Not even you.

Jethro I was busy at the time.

Tyrone Yeah, yeah.

*

Jethro Betsy?

Betsy Yes?

Jethro You want to play a game?

Betsy No.

Jethro Beautiful flowers.

Betsy Aren't they nice? What kind of game?

Jethro I don't know. Cards, maybe? Or dice?

Betsy My clothes stay on, no matter what.

Jethro Oh. I know. What flowers are they?

Betsy Some kind of Lily. Did you walk today?

Jethro A little bit.

Betsy You must walk. A little more each day. Knock yourself out.

Jethro I know. I tried.

Betsy Exercises, as well?

Jethro Yes.

Betsy Good. What do you want for lunch? Chicken salad, yogurt, and berries.

Jethro Sounds good.

Betsy Good.

Jethro Amanda.

Betsy Amanda?

Jethro She wants me to hire a bookkeeper, a pro.

Betsy And fire me?

Jethro Yes.

Betsy And who pays for that?

Jethro She will.

Betsy She thinks I'm trying to rob you.

Jethro Correct.

Betsy I'm not!

Jethro Your life is already too complicated by strange ideas, like space aliens, and I'm the one who finances it. And not only that, but you also measure my vodka—you sneak in here and measure how much vodka I drink before dinner, two fingers, three fingers, whatever, and then you tell the world about it!

Betsy I don't tell anyone anything, Jethro. I'm not innocent, but I'm not doing anything harmful or selfish. You need to be monitored. You could have a conniption or a heart attack and fall over dead. Who made such an arrangement of parts, where people stick their slimy bodies into each other? Reproduction? It's disgusting. Listen, I have some news for you, Jethro. You want to hear it or not?

Jethro Not.

Betsy There's this guy, Brad, he wants me to go out into the wilderness with him.

Jethro There is no wilderness no more.

Betsy He wants to give me massages and play chess with me.

Jethro What's he paying you?

Betsy I didn't agree to go with him yet.

Jethro I'll double it, whatever he's paying you.

Betsy Never mind. Don't worry.

Jethro Is there a subject named Trent?

Betsy There is. He followed me around. He kept staring at me in the laundromat. I said to the person next to me: "The culture of the United States has deteriorated markedly. How so? Your private parts are no longer private. They are available for scrutiny to any cowboy who looks at your crotch." I don't think that's right. Everything becomes genitalia. It's repulsive. Why do the Arabs imprison their women in black? Why? Because all they can see is undercover, deprived of air. They're pussy-whipped, the whole lot of them. Putting their women in black fabric, houses without doors.

Jethro That's stinking clothes in the night. That's got to be in our report, how the Arabs treat their women.

Betsy Uh-oh. Here comes someone in a wheelchair. I don't think she likes you.

Jethro It can't be!

Lady It's me, Jethro, your living nightmare. Remember the hardhat hiding in the sewer—

Jethro Who?

Lady The battle under the city of New York for power and influence, while the ocean rises to snatch you.

Jethro What hardhat?

Lady You have one choice. Kill yourself or die in a home. And tell your friend Tyrone to take his fateful exposition into the void.

Jethro Wait! What hard hat?

Lady A battle in the sewer with a giant rat. Ha, ha. *(Returns upstage.)*

Jethro You saw her?

Betsy I did.

Jethro You heard what she said?

Betsy It's mystifying.

Jethro I told you about those ladies in wheelchairs selling dope in front of my meeting.

Betsy Yes.

Jethro Became quite a gathering place for the down and the dirty. Big obese ladies in mechanized wheelchairs selling dope on the corner.

Betsy Right.

Jethro Then there's the men in hard hats, resenting the elite. So, she's harping on an image of them, maybe, reminding her of hated masculine power. Which is not me—I'm a harmless intellectual. While the radiomen spew their stupid lies for money.

Betsy Radiomen?

Jethro Daily! Shooting their mouths off! Creating chaos!

Betsy Calm down.

Jethro They should be lined up against a wall and shot. And that's where the Lady in the Wheelchair gets her ideas. The radiomen. I'll tell you, it's retaliation. Why?

Betsy I give up. Why?

Jethro She offered the greatest sex possible on this Earth and I turned her down, period. What do you think of that?

Betsy I don't know what to think, Jethro.

Betsy *He's dreaming while thinking. Keeping his dick covered. Backing away. There are demonized subspecies in her sub-imagination. Hardhats and radiomen.* Jethro. I hate to say it. Your personal decline is not the species' decline.

Jethro I think it is. People are grown more stupid with time apparently, electing a criminal con artist sleazebag to the presidency of the United States. The orange-haired president is just a symptom. A pig in garbage. Lies fill the air like carbon.

Tyrone There was a man in my childhood who lived in a clearing in the woods, Mr. Cross, he'd been a social studies teacher at the high school and now he was living in a stinky clearing in the forest. And there was another man I knew, a mild-mannered professor, a quiet, intelligent guy. One day he vanished. They said he'd walked down a path into the wild and was never seen again.

Constanza I have data on the wheelchair lady—she's a cripple with a lot of political power, apparently. The banks. The lawyers. The card accounts. She thinks she's in charge of the government—clowns running into the front of the bus and running out of the back of the bus. And the bus is going down into the crevices of the earth. The data is winding around the planet like yarn. Pretty soon it will strangle Mankind. Drugs and alcohol and old age and driving at night in the rain.

Tyrone I'm nearing the end and I have no money.

Constanza One problem is loneliness, and another is fear. I keep all my doors locked and I'm buying a dog. People don't realize all the poverty in this land. People sleep in their cars or under bridges. I'm lucky I got my little house here. You think I'm joking about the Commies, but I'm not. People don't know how to talk to each other. I don't blame you, Tyrone. Your life is coming to an end. It's either walking away or opening fire, randomly.

Tyrone Thanks, Constanza.

Constanza Facts are free. Facts are for nothing. There is not enough sense out there to make change from a dollar, especially American or Indonesian, and I could go on. All they know how to do is rob and steal and get blood flowing out of people and into pipes and ditches.

Tyrone Dark, Constanza.

Constanza Facts, Tyrone.

Betsy I guess your dad is about ready to move on into a cave and long days and nights of meditation.

Amanda I guess. They couldn't be more different, Jethro and my dad.

Tyrone You grew up a rich kid, Jethro, a mama's boy, a smart aleck. An elite type of Jew. Me, I'm trash. I got lucky. I had good teachers, they pushed me forward, they found a path for me. But we will always be estranged, you and me. No harm, no foul, but the class thing is like an invisible membrane separating us for good.

Jethro It's called resentment, Tyrone.

Tyrone It's called self-love, Jethro, self-love, and condescension. I'll be on my way, Amanda. You know how to take care of yourself. You know what's what. No drugs, no haphazard sex.

Amanda Yeah, yeah.

Tyrone I won't be in touch, but you'll feel me.

Amanda That makes no sense, dad.

Betsy I'm up for a truce if you are.

Amanda Definitely.

Betsy Maybe we'll run into each other again.

Amanda On the barricades.

Betsy There you go.

*

Jethro *I have trouble sleeping. Bad dreams, aching an invisible bone, a disturbed mind. As though a judgment was looking down into my soul like the old Hebrew God, implacable and close. I see all my lies and mistakes and ladies in wheelchairs selling dope and torture in the deserts of the spinning Earth. Spinning. And then, for a moment, as the Sun was starting to rise, I saw that all was energy, all life and movement was Energy, Life was*

Energy, the Universe was an expression of Energy, which cannot die, and I slept the sleep of Angels for a moment and haven't yet completely forgotten.

Tyrone *A word to Elaine, my first, and Diana, of the silky skin, and Zoe, her keen sensitivity, and Arlene, and Judith, and Amy of the green, silk dress, and all those I've since forgotten. I loved you all.*

Jethro I'm sure they will all appreciate your parting comments, Tyrone, with tears and laughter.

Tyrone Fuck you, Jethro.

*

Constanza I've interviewed a lot of people, Jethro, a lot of people, and I have to say that I'm depressed by it all. Incidents people have told me—shit hard to believe. I don't want to discuss it. Born into hellholes. Raised by ogres. Cutting up bodies. Alive. Live bodies. *(Lady in Wheelchair approaches.)* Uh-oh.

Lady Time's up.

Constanza Why?

Lady He's a junkie and an alcoholic.

Betsy No, he isn't.

Lady And a blowhard preacher to boot.

Constanza No, he isn't. He's Jewish.

Lady It's that or suicide.

Jethro Oh, come on.

Lady Look at your erratic behavior, going around asking people things.

Jethro We're gathering data.

Lady *Data, indeed. I'd like to see him confined in a safe place, like a hostel or a prison. I do have the power to put people away. Where they belong. Why? Because the world is led by a bunch of uncircumcised dickheads.*

Constanza Is that it, Lady?

Lady No. I have more. I have opinions. I have ideas. I have money. I have taste. I have connections. I have wants and desires.

Constanza Congratulations.

Lady Nothing's wrong with me. I have a loose pebble in my knee. I'm a junkie. I live happily in a wheelchair. I sell junk to my people. I get money from the government. I used to be beautiful, but now it's pointless. You'll be glad and Jethro will be glad. That you interviewed me, that you found me lounging in his territory, but there's no use in filing a report.

Constanza Thank you, very much.

Lady Don't thank me. I hate that. In the meantime, his love life turns to mud, his income evaporates, he becomes confined to an old age home, and suicide is his only other option. Furthermore, I am a walking tirade. Mankind is on its last bowel movement. And these are the Last Days.

Jethro Wait. I had a dream last night. I don't know where I was. Seemed like New York City. Somewhere dark and dangerous, but full of promise. I was there for a purpose which was somehow connected to a marriage. There was a beautiful woman there, still young, light-haired—face indistinct, but radiant with the premise of Happiness and Love. It was she who was getting married. It was unclear what I was doing there exactly, but there was an unspoken implication that I was there for her. I could never see her face. It was vague, indistinct, like I said, but loving. Then things began to get in the way or to go awkwardly wrong. It's like we were sliding toward each other, but a wall of gravity kept us apart. There was an invisible wall between us, and we couldn't make it through. We kept trying for a while, rolling around and losing force, until somehow the entire image faded heavily into the dark.

*

Tyrone *Jethro thinks about his situation. It's a kind of light mourning for all our losses. The disappointments and failures, the lack of love in his life. Disillusionment and ego fantasies. Real talent realized too late. The psychological damage. Like growing up under a lid instead of a sky. You will lose and you will fail, that's the way it is, beneath the words, beneath the ideas or the pictures and all the rest of the phony solutions, including women and drugs and therapies and the constant American pathetic stupidities of which he was an inevitable tiny part. And now it's all lost to degenerate animals. What good did I do? You want to die deaf and dumb, Tyrone? In this horrible place?*

Amanda *My dad walked. He took the last of his pills, drank a glass of red wine, hitched up his trousers, put on his good boots, and walked. My mother almost broke him—get the fuck out you piece of shit!*

Lady You police of shit!

Tyrone They let me out of re-hab early and I disappeared for a while, putting humpty-dumpty together again. I had just enough self-esteem. Back in Santa-Monica she said they were going away. and I said I'm not going with you. And they left. Amanda waved to me through the back window of the car. I remember standing there amid the boxes of books and papers and trash in the empty living room. Standing there.

Amanda Bye, bye.

Tyrone I tell my students, persevere, remember yourselves, you'll catch murder and mayhem out there in the field.

Lady Remember, fool.

Jethro *To sum up. I give it ten or fifteen years before the planet burns to a cinder or the water runs out and there's not enough oxygen to breathe. This is because the right-wing in America is triumphant and they can't see what's happening around them. And the voting patriots in the Midwest are too dumb to notice what they're doing when they support these people. So much for Democracy. And they're ugly, these people, men, and women both. So, get in your good times, but don't go crazy. Saw a TV show last night about the Sacred, a lot of it was about the fear of Death. Handle it that way. Energy cannot die, basically. There's a certain amount and you got some and so you get to go on. Think of it accordingly. So much for the data.*

Tyrone *Cold. Want to be in someone's arms. It was cold. Freezing air came down straight from the Arctic, down through the Catskills, and into the Brooklyn canyons.*

I'm thinking of Rockaway Avenue in particular. IRT. New Lots. And now I'm overcome, I can't go on... Snow was over my head. Wind was blowing into my face. Slush was in my galoshes. I had to change at Atlantic Avenue and go back the other way, toward Flatbush. Cold zigzagged trip on the fucking subway. Nowadays, nearing the end, I have a new direction and a new aim.

Jethro *They took me for a blood-test the other day. The girl behind the counter was speaking her thoughts out loud. She wasn't discerning, what she should say or not say. Talking, talking. Then a little Mexican guy wearing red shorts comes in and starts cursing about a fax. He's got welts and boils on his legs. He's cursing and cursing, in broken English, and nobody reacts. Not the girls or the nurses or the people waiting for their blood tests, like they're waiting for their fixes. Quiet, patient, motionless. This is all going on and nobody looks at anyone else. Nobody seemed to know anything about themselves. They were taking care of their bodies, and that's all they knew. And of even that, they weren't sure, because the body changes. It gets sick and breaks and then they're buried in the ground. They were bewildered. The guy in the red shorts, seeing that nobody was paying attention to him, started yelling into his phone.*

(Blackout)

THE END

DEATH SKY ABOVE

A PLAY

A hanging figure rigged up in a parachute—Big Head—Name's Painter. Hangs a few feet above the auditorium. Periodically he is hoisted up. There is a shill in the audience who makes remarks.

Hoists chains (loud winch SOUND). Crow Dog hoists the chain upward. And bangs the big Pueblo-style DRUM.

Painter I'm on my way back from Chiapas, Mexico, hallucinating devils through the cloudy sky. I weighed about ninety pounds, having got sick with amoebic dysentery and hepatitis B while kicking heroin in San Cristobal, a hundred miles north of armed guerillas in the jungle below, who are still down there fighting off the white landlords and Indian killers. They land me in a hospital in Manhattan, fearful for my life, so they make up their small minds—since I had been a junkie in New York City—to put me on methadone! Why? Because all junkies are methadone eaters. No, they were afraid I wasn't going to eat and therefore die there like a piece of limp shit in a tall tower. So they built me up to 120 mg a day, which was 3 biscuits dissolved in something like Gatorade and sent me home to Brooklyn where for months I could only eat pound cake and peaches. Everything else I threw up. I had to get up at five in the morning every day to take the subway to South Ferry, where I would get in line with the rest of the sick and raspy vomitatious junkies lined up at the window. You had to drink up right there and come back the next morning. This went on for months. I bloated up from the methadone and the pound cake. I can't believe this all happened in real life. Since I had a high recommendation from the minister of the St. Mark's Church and I may have gotten a grant or something, I finally talked my "counselor" into letting me pick up twice a week instead of every day and then I talked him into once a week and I started cutting down on the methadone, which was making me feel like a large insect.

Crow Dog I'm going to tell you what I think. I'm going to tell you what I really think. This is what I think. We live in a bad country. We already live there. You see them clouds? Take a good look. Look at them horses! They gallop the dust!

Painter This was like when I was flying through the air on a plane. Looked down and saw horses and clouds.

Crow Dog Firewater and the long guns!

Painter I was still on the plane, trying to drink a whiskey.

Crow Dog We walked for seven hundred miles and then we couldn't walk anymore. A hymn for the dead and the dying. We knew what the dust was. We ate the dust. It was us. Our shadows were gone, they had joined the sky.

Painter I think I was still on the plane at that time, sick as a dog and throwing up again, finally.

Crow Dog You see them dark clouds?

Painter I said to Crow Dog: Come live with me and I'll protect your soul. Crow Dog is an old friend of mine who says he is a war chief of a California Indian tribe, but who is in reality a large and scary Black man who calls himself Crow Dog. He grew up on 116th street and takes no shit from white people, me being the only exception.

Crow Dog You can't protect my soul, I ain't got no soul. I ain't got no soul and I don't believe in anything.

Painter I am hanging, hanging in the sky tied up in a parachute. As I endure yet even more and more suffering from Life's endless injustices. I'm trying to take a sitting position now and I don't feel sorry for myself.

Crow Dog I'll smite you with my war club. No one has it worse than the American Indian.

Painter Crow Dog is my only friend besides the St. Mark's Church and when he hears of my troubles he promptly heads back to the city from Wyoming with his walking stick and his robe and bells on his ankles and a weird fur hat. I didn't see him for months. Meanwhile, it was all peaches and pound cake and methadone. Then Karen showed up. Karen had a crush on me in high school. Who am I to have a crush on, thought I, I am not worthy of crushes or a solid meal. All I ever wanted was to get high. So I wasn't quite aware. Karen was, though. What a sweetheart. We spent a few days together. Having sex and walking in the park and walking to the river, and walking downtown and having sex, and then she went back to Hurleyville.

Crow Dog You should have married that girl, Painter, and got a job.

Painter I never realized. I should have married her, then and there, and lived a happy life teaching English in the Catskills. But it was not to be. I'm no good at relationships. I was ruined in childhood.

Crow Dog Don't worry, he's not gonna tell you about it.

Painter But I never did shoot up again, if that's what you're thinking. I kept saving up on the methadone, thinking I was going to beat it one day, come hell or high water. Then I got another miracle grant and went back to Mexico. This time it was the Yucatán, to a town called Progreso. All the people were my size, and everything was copacetic. I had a Lebanese connection named Moyo, who got me a weekly carton of Lucky Strikes and a bottle of good Cuban rum, and I kept on reducing my methadone count until the five months in Paradise came sadly to an end.We took a ferry from Campeche to Miami, and I still had a stash of methadone. Approaching Miami, I fearfully threw the stash down the toilet. Give us a hoist, Crow Dog! Hoist!

(Hoist) (LOUD)

Crow Dog HOIST!

(DRUM)

Crow Dog Drum. Hoisted. Good! You're hoisted. We'll keep on hoisting you. We'll hoist you till the poison's gone and you got your spirits back.

Painter Thank you, Dog! I must be feet off the ground!

Crow Dog This here is an ancient ceremony you know nothing about. Mainly, it's an adaptation of our own devising based on the piercing ceremony of the Lakota tribe, which you know nothing about and about which you know nothing. You see here a parachute and a rope and a winch and that's all I'll say. We're on our way.

Painter Where, say?

Crow Dog UP. By inches. Wait and see. HOIST HIM, says I who know. I have watched the shadows come and go. Thoughts and wishes, dreams and bitches, whole seances with witches.

Painter I don't know what a wish is. Been meaning to ask. Just didn't want to sound stupid or illiterate.

Crow Dog You think people don't notice, but they do. They know everything about you. A drug addict and a drunk. A sexless wonder rising into the sky in a rig. Chaste he is, and his bones are broken. Arthritic hips, three vertebrates gone with the wind. Head nowhere it used to be. Where is it? Could be in pieces, parts of it overheated. Melted like wax, rubbed out, like clay. Looks like a dot in the sky, limbs attached by rubber bands. We'll hoist him up and he'll charge into the fray and attack the Attacker. He's our boy. We call him the twitter tweet from Hell.

Painter Oh, no! If it wasn't so sad, it'd be a joke.

Crow Dog No joke. Where I come from, the hubris is funny until they take your scalp. Cut your hair off. Cut your ears off. Dig a bone into your kidney. Put a hot wire up your dick. Now, that's elemental, nothing to cry about. Fat pig-like creature with orange hair. You gotta see it to believe it. Watcha doin' up there, my friend?

Painter I'm praying to the Four Directions, Crow.

Crow Dog Wait a minute, I'll get my drum.

Painter I thought you said gun. I thought you said wait a minute I'll get my gun.

Crow Dog Drum!

Painter HOIST!

(Hoist) (LOUD)

Crow Dog HOIST!

Painter Not so loud!

Crow Dog It's the winch!

Painter Wait a minute.

Crow Dog Yeah?

Painter My guts appear to be falling onto the orchestra.

Crow Dog Yeah?

Painter I hope they don't hit nobody.

Crow Dog Who cares?

Painter The belt is too tight. It is squeezing my gut.

Crow Dog Loosen the belt. You got any brains left up there?

Painter My I.Q. is over 200. Figure that one out. I never even took any tests. I read a lot in my room. They put me right into an honors class at Brooklyn College. I started walking down Rockaway Avenue and ended up on Miami Beach. Go figure. HOIST!

Crow Dog Wait a minute!

Painter HOIST! It'll loosen the rig.

Crow Dog No it won't. Just the opposite. *(To Audience)* He was a kosher busboy in Miami Beach.

Painter HOIST!

(Hoist)

Crow Dog HOIST! *(Pause)*

Painter What'd you do, Crow?

Crow Dog I hoisted.

Painter No, I meant before that, in ordinary life.

Crow Dog I scalped him. Then I cut the top of his head off. Then I kicked his teeth in. Then I sawed off his jaw.

Painter What else?

Crow Dog Are you being a wise guy now?

Painter No.

Crow Dog Do you really care?

Painter No.

Crow Dog I cut his head off and threw it into the river.

Painter Hit the drum. Loud.

(Drum)

Painter Louder!

DRUM!

Crow Dog Yeah. The eels ate him.

Aud *He's dripping all over me. I'd like an explanation.*

Crow Dog You want an explanation?

Aud *You hard of hearing?*

Crow Dog You want an explanation? Yes or NO.

Aud *Yes!*

Crow Dog Okay. Here's the explanation. *(He pisses on him.)*

Aud *You SONOFABITCH!*

Painter Give him his money back and tell him to go home.

Crow Dog What's that?

Painter Give him his money back and tell him to go home.

Crow Dog Would you like your money back, sir?

Aud *Yes, and I'd like some fresh clothes, please.*

Crow Dog That was not piss, that was plain water, it'll dry in a minute.

Painter And we don't have fresh clothes around here.

Crow Dog Do you still want your money back? Yes or no?

Aud *No. I want to see what happens next.*

Crow Dog Everything's happened already. Everything has already happened. What did you expect?

Aud *What about the poor fellow hanging above us?*

Painter HOIST!

(HOIST)

Crow Dog HOIST!

Aud *Loud. That's loud!*

Painter LOUDER!

(HOIST)

Crow Dog *HOIST! (Painter RISES HIGHER.)*

(DRUM)

Painter DRUM!

Crow Dog Good!

Painter Stand up Crow Dog and show 'em your REAL dick!

Crow Dog No thanks. I'm in a good posture here and I won't move. Change it now and I'll never find it again. Thanks a lot.

Aud *I DON'T WANT TO SEE HIS REAL DICK, IF YOU DON'T MIND.*

Painter You'd be astounded.

Crow Dog You'd be amazed.

Painter You'll be shocked!

Crow Dog I got other things to do right now.

Aud *Thank God.*

Painter HOIST!

Crow Dog DRUM! Good!

Painter Give him an explanation.

Crow Dog I already gave him an explanation.

Painter Give him another one.

Crow Dog I used a hose, okay? I used a fucking hose!

Aud *Okay! Say more!*

Painter Give him another one. The man paid for his ticket.

Crow Dog Motherfucker can't move further than an electrical impulse. You got that? Then it stops and turns his hair orange. You got that? Then I use his hair as bait.

Aud *For what?*

Crow Dog To catch eels. You like that? You like eels? If they bite you, you get a shock. They're electrified. Sky too, electrocution in the sky. Like lightning. Motherfuckers got off a boat and put us in cages and poked around and electrocuted. Now my friend is hooked up and rising. You maybe are wondering why.

Aud *Why?*

Crow Dog You weren't paying attention. I used a certain word, and you weren't paying attention. Think. What was the word? *(Silence)*

Painter BAIT!

Crow Dog Fine. Are you happy now, Painter?

Aud *I still don't get it.*

Crow Dog I will give you a final explanation. See if you can follow.

Aud *I will try my best.*

Crow Dog Good. There is a monster haunting the Valley. He is the pink pig with orange hair who flies above us. He is made of air and a rubber cones—in other words, he farts his way around looking for tufts of orange that he confuses with pizza. You get that?

Aud *NO!*

Crow Dog In other words, he hangs around up there like a giant balloon, and we are going to catch him with a pointed lodge pole topped with a tuft of orange hair.

Painter He farts all over us, the sonofabitch!

Aud *You just made that up!*

Painter Hoist!

(HOIST)

Painter HOIST!

Crow Dog Good!

(DRUM)

Painter DRUM!

Crow Dog Good!

Painter Loud enough? High enough?

Crow Dog No, but hold up a minute. They're running for the exits! They're running for the doors! They're running for the cops! Come back and he'll explain everything that can be explained!

Painter Speak for yourself, Crow.

Crow Dog Come on back!

Painter Hit that fucking drum, Crow Dog!

(DRUM)

Crow Dog DRUM!

Painter Good. I'll turn my eyes on. How about that? How 'bout I turn my eyes on?

Crow Dog Gaw head!

Painter I'll turn my eyes on!

Crow Dog Turn 'em on!

Painter Cause they're electrified! What do you think of that?

Crow Dog Turn 'em on!

Painter Bring 'em back, Crow! Ger them back in here! There'll be no refunds!

Crow Dog There'll be no refunds!

Aud *This better be good!*

Painter What color? What color you like? You like brown?

Aud *NO!*

Painter You like black?

Aud *NO!*

Painter Green?

Crow Dog MAYBE?

Painter BLUE? You like blue? How 'bout BLUE? Okay, let's try RED—What do you say to RED?

Aud *BLUE!*

Painter Okay—BLUE! Here we go, BLUE!

(His big eyes turn blue!)

Crow Dog What do you think of that? That's fuckin' amazing! Looks great! His head is fucked up, but his eyes are blue!

Aud *I think it looks nice.*

Crow Dog Just don't piss anymore or spit or spittle or fart or fuckle or do anything else. You can turn your eyes blue, but don't do anything else.

Painter Right!

(HOIST)

Painter HOIST!

Crow Dog Good!

(DRUM)

Painter DRUM! Good!

Crow Dog And don't take a shit up there!

Painter That reminds me. I saw a movie once. They put a whole bunch of people in the hold of a ship and then they dumped a truck full of shit on 'em! Saw it in a movie. I thought, holy shit, I hope that never happens to me. But of course it did, it happened to yours truly, so I'm perfectly capable of it because I saw it happen in a movie and then it happened to me. Okay, I'm gonna turn my eyes off now.

(He turns off his eyes!)

Aud *What the fuck! What the fuck! You can't see shit! You can't see shit! Turn on the lights! Turn on the fuckin' lights!*

Crow Dog I hit the wrong switch, okay? HOIST!

(HOIST)

Painter HOIST!

Crow Dog Good!

Painter DRUM!

Crow Dog Good!

Painter You're lit, Crow Dog!

Crow Dog I can tell. So he figured he'd blow off half the world and keep the rest for himself. That's my explanation. He is pink as a pig and large as a blimp and has orange hair.

Painter Stand up and show 'em your dick, Crow Dog.

Crow Dog No.

Painter He wears a dick and an eagle feather and a blanket. What the fuck you call that? Fuckin' Indian, he'll eat anything that crawls.

Aud *Here comes something.*

Painter That's a spider.

Aud *Don't eat the spider! Oh, no!*

Painter He ate it already.

Aud *Oh, no!*

Crow Dog He got like tiny daggers for eyes. I was watching him looking at a fella with a big phony grin, he's lookin' at the fella, he's in profile, an' he smiles like I hate you, you hateful piece of shit, I absolutely hate you, and then he turns to the CAMERA, and he makes another face—it's like sliding into a crash, you could hear the ships colliding. You could see he'd just about kill anybody because everybody was a scumbag beneath him, but he didn't do it out of the goodness of his heart.

Painter It's because of the CAMERA. I'll explain later.

Aud *Why are you hoisting him up there? Why are you hoisting that fella up into the air? Why are you doing that?*

(HOIST)

Painter HOIST!

Crow Dog Good!

(DRUM)

Crow Dog DRUM!

Painter Good. Because he's garbage, pure and simple. You got that? Because we are going to puncture him with a lodge pole and the air will escape, a wind which will contain an aroma, a stink such as never before been stunk on earth, a—what's the word I'm looking for here?

Aud *Miasma?*

Painter Miasma! Exactly, a cloud and a wind and a fog and a stink such as has never been seen on earth!

Aud *I'm getting out of here!*

Painter This task has been given us because we are warriors of the Indigenous peoples of America.

Crow Dog Actually, I'm the only warrior around here.

Aud *Good-bye and good luck!*

Painter Give him his money back. Give him all his fucking money back. Every dime. Every filthy dollar. Give it back.

Crow Dog Okay.

(MONEY FALLS FROM ABOVE!)

Aud *I don't want no money back!*

Crow Dog What's wrong with you? You don't know what money is? Money is LIFE, you stupid jerk!

Aud *What about the CAMERA?*

Painter Give him his money back, and we ain't answering no questions. We are going to dispose of this specimen, this humongous pink pig, by throwing him into the celestial garbage dump. What do you think of that?

Aud *What about the CAMERA?*

Crow Dog All right, I'll tell you—pick up our money and I'll tell you. Pick up the money. Good.

Painter Tell him to give the money back first.

Crow Dog Give the money back first. Just pretend. Good. Very good.

Aud *And now for the explanation!*

Painter I'm going to get as high as I can before I shit on all of you. What do you think of that?

Crow Dog He forgot what the subject of the conversation was.

Painter Right. And we don't care what you think.

Crow Dog Let's get a little higher, John.

Aud *John?*

(HOIST)

Crow Dog HOIST!

Painter Good.

(DRUM)

Crow Dog DRUM!

Painter Good.

Aud *CAMERA!*

Painter Ah. What's the word I'm looking for, Crow?

Crow Dog BAIT.

Painter Bait. Exactly. Bait.

Aud *But what does it mean?*

Painter Bait means bait. What else could it mean? You get that?

Crow Dog So there you have it.

Aud *Why?*

Crow Dog Because half the world eats shit and the other half eats oysters. Because our fat friend doesn't realize he's got mercury in his feet, shit for brains, and maggots in his liver.

Aud *What are ya gonna do with him?*

Crow Dog We're gonna puncture him and skin him and shoot his teeth up to the nearest starry garbage dump. I hope you don't go out there with me because you might get one of his contagions. We were talking about that earlier, John and I, mortal diseases and ancient beliefs and weird religions, like Zoroastrianism or Fascism. But mainly it's contagious. The point is that it's contagious. Fascism is the one.

Painter You can't go. Too many strange illnesses up there and it's dark and the gravity is fucked up in a whirl. Anyway, you can't go.

Crow Dog I'm not going either.

Painter Siddown, Crow.

Crow Dog No.

Painter Okay, don't siddown. Time for a hoist?

Crow Dog Not yet. Give it a minute.

Painter I'll give it a minute. Okay, go!

(HOIST)

Painter HOIST!

Crow Dog Good.

(DRUM)

Painter DRUM!

Crow Dog Good. People like to be positive and think good thoughts, especially about theirselves, but it's too late for that now because the negative particles are in the air. They are in the air and they perculate. They perculate. That's what they like to do. So you got people with mustachios being positive and having happy thoughts while inside the negative particles are busy eating their livers.

Painter Yikes.

Crow Dog That's all I'm saying.

Painter You didn't say anything.

Crow Dog I'm telling you—every time I hit the drum, we're that much closer!

Painter To what?

Crow Dog OBLIVION. The pink pig will lead the way. He'll stink up the other half of the world and lead us on our merry way.

Aud *May I ask, sir, what's the Drum got to do with it?*

Crow Dog John?

Painter This guy is a complete idiot. You better explain, Crow Dog.

Crow Dog I have no explanation.

Painter Give us an interpretation, then.

Crow Dog I have no interpretation.

Painter Tell us what it means, then.

Crow Dog I don't know what it means. There's nothing below the South Pole. That means there was Nothing until there was Something, which blew the whole thing to smithereens and now we're racing toward the boundary—however, there is no Boundary. We're going a mile a minute from Nothing to Nothing, on the back of a pink pig.

Aud *He didn't give me an answer!*

Painter There is no answer. You can try. You're welcome to try.

Kill the pig, maybe. Use a shotgun maybe. No discounts, I'm afraid, like we told you.

Aud *That ain't it!*

Painter Well, take a hike then! Make one up, Crow Dog, that'll work for ya. Don't get stressed by it, easy does it, do it easily, like water flowing from a rock. Gaw head.

Crow Dog Okay. The Drum is Magic. It is made of hydrogen and helium and spontaneous combustion. You wanna hear it? Here we go!

(HOIST)

HOIST!

Good!

(DRUM)

DRUM!

Crow Dog Good! There you go. And there's no afterlife. Don't even think about it. Big Daddy is not there to welcome you into Paradise. Those of you who like to splatter blood all over the woods and the hills—Fuhgeddaboudit. Especially you, with your sharia salami and your bloody hatchets.

Aud *Whoa!*

Painter We are not kidding, the baseline or the pre-thought that is to say the background noise of the noise is: KILL THE JEWS, and so it will remain, unless there's some kind of evolutionary process coming from the stars in this absolutely meaningless arrangement of galaxies and stars signifying Nothing as they speed away. And so we have set our trap, and we are ready, and have just enough time and you can run away if you want to just make it fast and don't leave any of your crap around.

Crow Dog Time for a HOIST.

Painter Yo. Go!

Wait a minute. So it's time for not believing all the bullshit we are used to believing. I'm talking about myself now, which is equally Nothing to the Nothing we find when we look, but hardly see anything when we do look, so things go on as they are forever and ever where Nothing is seen and Nothing is heard. I'm in a lot of pain now, physically, and I realize, in spite of that, that you don't give a rat's ass one way or another. Hell of a way to be a theater Patron. Anyway, gaw head Crow Dog, do your shit.

(HOIST)

Crow Dog HOIST!

(DRUM)

DRUM!

Good!

(DRUM)

Crow Dog Good. You are a Nothing species and Nothing is going to come from it but more Destructive Nothing and so-called Nature couldn't care less about Nothing. It just does its thing. Great. I'm going to piss on you now, and I don't care what you think about it, because you are incapable of actual Thought.

Painter Thanks, Crow. I'll do it. While I try to get my fly open.

Crow Dog You couldn't do it before.

Painter Never mind. We are dealing now with TIME. Time for you to go fuck yourselves, whatever that means, whoever you are, the finest, the brilliant, the hotshot banana heads, the white-eyes, the stupefied, the dumb, the illiterates. So, I'll ponder that.

Aud You'll ponder what?

Painter TIME.

Crow Dog Tell them to get out of the way. GET OUT OF THE WAY. HE'S NOT PONDERING, HE'S PREPARING TO TAKE A PISS.

Aud *WHAT ARE YOU DOING UP THERE?*

Painter I CAN'T GET MY FLY OPEN. I HATE THAT. WHY IS THAT? WHY CAN'T I OPEN THINGS? I RESENT THAT. THERE'S A CINCH IN THE WAY HERE, OR A STRAP, OR A BELT, OR A BUTTON, OR A ZIPPER, I DON'T KNOW WHAT THE FUCK IT IS. AND I DRIP, YOU GET OLD AND YOU CAN'T CONTROL YOUR OPERATIONS ANYMORE. LEAKAGE OCCURS. I DON'T THINK THAT'S FAIR.

Crow Dog It's not fair. Get used to it.

Painter I'M GOING TO GO AHEAD AND PISS. IT'LL DRIP ALL OVER YOU UNLESS YOU GET OUT OF THE WAY IN A HURRY.

Crow Dog Wait! It's not fair, hold it in, hold it in, I mean, not fair to them or me either because I'm safe on stage with my sage and cedar for company and my Pueblo Drum—I got nothing to worry about but a bad taste in the morning. What happened to the good old days, you Freak, where you used to say a good line and a good line would be in the answer and a character appeared who wasn't acting like Spider Man but had a real character and a problem to be solved? What happened to all that?

Painter It went away with the winged pink pig. He took it all away in favor of gold towers and phony jobs and the electrified soybeans and the shit I'm going to lay on you any minute now. It's on its way.

Aud *Oh, no! Please!*

Crow Dog HE'S LOSING IT NOW. DON'T PAY ANY MORE ATTENTION.

(HOIST)

HOIST!

Good.

(DRUM)

DRUM!

Piss!

Crow Dog Good! Then Karen showed up one day.

Voice of Karen *I just wanted to tell you—I had an abortion.*

Painter You had an abortion?

Karen I had an abortion.

Painter Where was I? New York City. What was I doing? Shooting up?

Karen WE HAD BEEN EVICTED!

Painter Good Grief. Now it was too late. What could I have been thinking? I could have lived a normal life, not strung up here on methadone EVICTED!

Crow Dog You could never have lived a normal life. Fuhgeddaboudit.

Painter THAT WAS Crow Dog. That was Crow Dog. You can tell because T's become D's. I could've married that girl and stayed in the Catskills and lived a normal life. Instead I was an evicted drug addict stranded in New York City. These two LGBT guys had bought a brownstone in Brooklyn for 18K and sold it for 3 mil and put my stuff in storage. All my seventies gear stolen, the leather cape, the leather jacket, the beaded headband. Hipster wear. So much for the Yucatán. Luckily I had a theater friend who had a farm, ee-eye-ee-eye-yo, and on that farm he had a tide, and the tide flew in on wheels, the fastest in the world. Otherwise it was dark and rainy all the night. And so it was in NOVA SCOTIA.

Painter Good. Nobody lived there. And if I hadn't told you yet, I'm telling you now: IF YOU WANT TO QUIT METHADONE YOU DO NOT START SUFFERING UNTIL A DAY OR TWO GO BY ON NOTHING AND THEN YOU START TO SUFFER. No, no. No, you do not cut down and cut back little by little and it gets better—in your imagination, anyway—you got down to nothing and that's when, that's right, the shit hits the fan. It's a lot like being hoisted by chains or dangled from a tall lodgepole with a hook in your chest. It's called *piercing*. Ask Crow Dog.

Crow Dog Yeah, it's like that. Tied to a Lodge Pole and swinging by your chest.

Painter And that's like only a day or two.

Crow Dog Yeah. They cut you down after a while and you drink a lot of apple juice. The older bingers disappear into the woods, and you don't see 'em for a year. They appear once a year later when it's time to watch you hang for a day or two. It's an honor and a privilege to let a Black guy or a Jew hang in the ceremony. But I quit after a while. Quit the hard suffering. Got my Indian name and kept my connections. Been in Sweat Lodges where it got to be a thousand degrees. After a while, my butt couldn't take it no more. A course, I'm eggzagerating, and I'm still on the Red Road. The Red Road is what they call the Way of Black Elk, the Lakota Way, or The Way of the Pipe, and I told my boy you get off that shit and sleep a whole night through and wake up and eat breakfast, I'll take you to a Sweat Lodge and you're done.

Painter Course they would have taken me anyway, any which way, could've been a serial murderer. They take crazed teenagers and demented old alcoholics. They'd have certainly taken me into the Lodge, but I imagined things. Purity of which does not any longer live on the Earth. Crow Dog is as sober as an oatmeal cookie, and he follows the Way and he had me fooled.

Crow Dog I'll say a few words. SAYS Crow Dog.

Painter DON'T YELL.

They'll take anybody, blotches up and down his veins,

scabby holes in his neck, thirteen dead men buried in his yard. That ain't it, ain't what it's about. It's 'bout evenin' up the score, had the Black bulls plowin' up in here by the Spanish, had raiding parties of Black warriors starvin' to death and eating raw babies' livers live. And it's the crime of all, which is being you in the first place. Crow Dog. Got the orange puppy with the size of a macaroni dick included for free, because he ain't made the Human Being no more, he be an orange pig. But mainly I been pissed on by the white zombies, the already dead white boys who like to lynch us hardy Black men with big cocks so we're practicing until our day is come and it's coming fast. You okay, white boy?

(HOIST) (LOUD)

HOIST!

Good!

(DRUM)

DRUM!

(LOUDER!)

Painter Good! Now they say I'm crazy. Whip it up that I'm a lunatic, can't hold two thoughts in my mind, one cancels out the other, and then they say I'm paranoid. Hear voices. Crazy old man. Sleeps in a parachute. It's true: lost the old zippy-de-do. Don't feel like doing much and sex is a horrifying prospect. What an operation. Time was, I couldn't think about nothing else. Now I just want a jiggly old Grandma who speaks Yiddish and makes chicken soup. But she died sixty-seven years ago. Maybe I am crazy. I feel like I'm wrapped in gauze. Revenge fantasies. The rock runs down the hill because he wants to and then he turns red with rage and attacks the worshipful Gestapo.

Crow Dog Go figure.

Painter I'll say a few words.

Crow Dog Gaw head, you old bird. Sounds like a crow cawing on a Brooklyn street. Totally inappropriate.

Painter Never mind. I don't feel like talking.

Crow Dog Okay. Sounds like a lost dog, a straggled dog.

Painter I declined already.

Crow Dog Go on, then.

Painter So I'm in Nova Scotia sick all day and night drinking black rum and finally I get a letter inviting me to Southern California. My girlfriend's grandmother died, and somebody has to take care of the house. Next thing we know we're in jail in Las Vegas. Woman is hollerin' at me and we both got drunk and ended in the hoosegow. Saved again by the Church. Let us out on a Monday and headed for the Eastern Sierras in a grey Mustang. So American.

Crow Dog Life is for the Immortals, the generation of Abraham. Everyone else goes to the shithouse.

Aud *Why did you say that?*

Painter I've figured it out, finally. Thank you for asking. Usually, in the Jewish, or even Christian, family, the Firstborn, the brightest Son, the talented One, the One with brains and a Future, such a person is prized and encouraged and even given something more to eat, if there is anything to eat, and more time to work, and his wit is encouraged and he is forgiven his faults, and so on. Not true in my case. In my case, it was the other way around. In my case, I was held responsible for the misfortunes of all, and all my Obedience and effort, intellectually and emotionally, was meant to give my parents solace and money and everything else that they dreamt was possible, even obligated, even ordained for them, without the troubling thought or the pangs of conscience—giving them the right to ask and expect obedience and tithing from the Firstborn, talented Son. Such an emotional arrangement has fucked me up for Life. And now I want to blame the Audience. And so, we will do what needs to be done.

Crow Dog Yeah. Hoist 'em up, the whole lot of 'em. But make sure you skin the pink pig with the orange hair. He cares about nothing but his macaroni-sized dick.

HOIST!

END

NO PLAY

—Are you going out, Jim?

—I'm going out.

—Hunting?

—Hunting.

—Good luck then.

—Thank you.

—In the office and the city?

—Yes.

—Kill the motherfuckers.

—Yes, I will.

—And what about the Wilsons downtown?

—What about them?

—They must be killed as well.

—I know.

—Onward.

—There's a protocol.

—So what?

—You can't do the culling out of hand.

—Why not?

—It's procedural.

—Kid can't talk, mother grovels in the plaza.

—Who is that?

—The Wilsons

—It's a shame.

—She was born good that one.

—She was.

—No one knows what happened there.

—Nothing happened there.

—Bad genes happened there.

—Far as we know.

—It's not important.

—What's important?

—The killing is important. Protect the good.

—Okay.

—Protect the holy.

—Right.

—Protect the bank.

—Of course.

—Get on it.

—There will be a hearing.

—What for?

—There is a relative, an Uncle John. He has his own show.

—What does he want?

—Fairness. Justice.

—Oh, come on.

—He's allowed to express his views.

—About you?

—Yes, and the procedure. It's lawful.

—Meanwhile. Don't let her sleep around. Mrs. Wilson.

—She's home arrested.

—Don't let any men in there.

—Of course not.

—We'll get progeny for sure.

—Yeah.

—Must kill them all then.

—How are you feeling, Jim?

—I feel like I want to throw someone out the office window.

—Hang in there.

—Forty-fifth floor. See the body splash on the pavement.

—The Uncle John is here.

—Blood and guts strewn about.

—He wants to talk.

—Let him talk.

—With you.

—I don't think so.

—It's the rule. One relative gets one shot. Live.

—Should be a firing squad. Set it up for everyone to see.

—She'll be hunted down as it is. We let her out and let her run for her life.

—So what does the Uncle want?

—A head start maybe, for his niece.

—I get it.

—Maybe not.

—Then what?

—A repeal, a reprise, a reevaluation of the evidence.

—We don't do that anymore. The genealogy is unpredictable. But we'll let her run. And then we'll shoot to kill.

—A head start then.

—We'll see. Let him come. Let him come in for an interview.

—How are you, dear?

—I'm fracked.

—I don't know what that means.

—In globs of plastics and rubber cement. Not good. Blown to smithereens. When the time comes. I'd like to fuck a young man with sense. I've been fucking around for years, and I haven't found one. Not one.

—It's over, dear. The hunt is on.

—Let it come.

—I'm trying to negotiate with the idiot savant whose name is Jim.

—Good luck, Uncle John.

—Thank you, Sarah. We'll get it reviewed or a head start.

—How long?

—Maybe a mile.

—A mile is good. Fucking robots clanking after me. Wired up dogs. Vengeful females.

—The rest of the family.

—Yeah?

—What do we do? They'll be also on the run.

—Head for the mountains. Cross the desert. Go out to sea.

—And you?

—The forest. I'll need at least a mile.

—And then?

—I have a spot in the hills. A sweet clearing in the woods, hard to find. I know it well and would be happy there.

—What will you do there, Sarah, in your glen?

—I'll start a school—arts and crafts for runaways. Perhaps song and dance as well.

—Well, Uncle John.

—Hello, Jim.

—What can I do for you? Speak English please. That is the language of our society.

—I know that.

—And its laws.

—Right.

—Speak up.

—How is Martha?

—Come on.

—Children well? Because that's the point. The gene pool. The moral good and so on.

—Yeah?

—There are doubts.

—There are no doubts.

—Something could sneak in, slide in, jump in, fly in, who knows?

—We have laws. We cull.

—My niece, as you know, as you recall, Sarah Wilson—

—Come on. We'll let the family go—wherever it wants, out of the country, goodbye and good luck, but we will kill your Sarah according to Law.

—Let's talk.

—We're talking.

—Law says the villain gets a good head start. Let her run.

—There is a virtual law built into the system.

—It's not a law. It's only a suggestion.

—Giving the accused and slandered the right to run for it.

—Laws are hard to come by John. Takes hard work and sacrifice. Time and effort. Good will and cooperation. We are not insects.

—I beg your pardon.

—Not Communists.

—I understand.

—A system that works for all Viewers regardless, laws and protocols and customs. Okay, where were we?

—Negotiation.

—Right.

—We submit to a certain rage sir on the part of my Sarah who likes to dance around like a dervish and has too many intimate relationships.

—So?

—Give her a couple miles.

—No. We go after her and we kill her right away so we can clean this thing up.

—Did we forget the Wilsons?

—We did.

—Let's not forget them.

—I'm sorry, dear.

—Leave us not forget them.

—Say more.

—Raggedy ones scurrying along like they were going to get away with it.

—Right.

—But we got them where we want them.

—They don't do like we do.

—No.

—Who knows what they're doing? They're on trial. They're not on screen.

—That's what I'm saying.

—Call the Judge.

—The Judge's gone up in a blaze.

—I heard.

—We have a way—how the world came to be, how our community is organized.

—We have our way of doing things.

—That's what I'm saying.

—Judge Dingo.

—He burned up in a barn fire.

—Sorry.

—Turned over a lamp while hiding.

—Why hiding?

—Can't say these things. It's the decency regulation.

—Move on.

—Generations to come, the genealogy of fate, so to speak.

—Yeah.

—Corruption breeds on itself like a mold.

—Yeah.

—Hunt the woman down, make an example.

—I will do that, sir.

—Jim.

—Martha.

—Office life becoming weird?

—Terrifying.

—How so?

—The boss wants us to get out there and kill some people.

—Oh.

—And not sit around playing games.

—Which people?

—Like the Wilsons.

—Do what you must do, Jim.

—And there's a money pot, a bassinet filled with money for any derring-do. You can imagine the competition.

—Insinuate.

—Yeah.

—And talk to people. Make friends with people and get them on the run. Plus, the madwoman bounding around dropping her water all over.

—What do you mean by that?

—It's an image.

—I see.

—Gutless wonders.

—Who is that?

—They're interviewing Uncle John live. Look—they keep on smiling. It could be the Black Death G-d forbid. Can't lose the Viewers. Don't upset the Viewers. They constitute the Republic.

—Right.

—We don't want to upset them. They're complicated. Hard to figure them out and follow through on the plan.

—I understand.

—That's what I'm saying.

—What's that?

—Separate them out. Snatch their kids.

—Who is this fellow Jim?

—Funny guy.

—Go on.

—He's made a fetish out of his self-image. A character he is playing. It's a form of schizophrenia in my view. So, he's like this weird performance of a person.

—Oh, my G-d.

—It's insecurity. It's like you don't feel sure if it's working. So, you step back and make proposals. James Dark. Jimmy Dark. It's the insecurity. There's nobody there essentially.

—Jim.

—He's dangerous.

—Fake, like he knows something.

—His wife's the power in those operations. Martha. A control freak.

—What operations?

—Public safety. Communications.

—I see.

—So, he has his proposals.

—Don't let him speak into the Camera.

—I don't know if I can do that. My powers are limited by the Constitution.

—And Judge Dingo is gone.

—Right.

—Keep an eye out. Maybe we kill this skunk. If we get a chance. If there's an opportunity.

—Will do.

—This is Uncle John talking to you direct. There is a woman running around town with her hair on fire. Stay home. Don't interfere. We've got the fire department out with the trucks and the hoses. Note that Judge Dingo's memorial has happened. Speaking of fire. We've got it on tape. You can't get drunk and throw a kerosene lamp into dry straw in an old barn, an antique old American barn. Was it intentional? We'll never know. He was a mountebank, a judge for show, for aggravating the common good. His fat simmered in the flames. Strike that. There'll be an election sometime soon. Do not gather. Stay home. We will call you when the time is established and then you can freely vote. This is not a dictatorship where one person decides who gets plenty and who gets none. We'll find a new Judge who can stand up to criticism and look good on your devices. Myself, I feel imperiled by technology. I could say more but I'll stop now. Thank you. Thank you very much. I just want to add right here—my niece, Miss Sarah Wilson, is irritating to some of you because of her independent spirit, her charm and her honest demeanor and her entertainment value, her joy in performance—you might deliberate on the envy factor in these proceedings, envy and the wish to harm, thank you. I'll say no more.

*

—What's this about Uncle John?

—He's fucking his niece.

—Come on.

—I saw the tape.

—Where does he get the balls?

—He appeared on TV and developed a following and there you have it. The Viewers decide.

—And his niece?

—She's quiet and docile.

—What do you think?

—I like her a lot. I like the way she walks. And that smile.

—She is alluring.

—She is alluring. But can she perform? Under stress?

—I see.

—Can she get that asshole off her unless of course she enjoys the whole thing.

—You're jealous.

—I mean, who is this person who thinks he can make proposals—how folks should live and die?

—He was elected by the Viewers.

—I'm not jealous. I really don't care. I want to do my job is all.

—It's hard. Power is hard. Especially if you don't know what you're doing.

—Thank you for that.

—There will be snipers.

—I know.

—Keep your head down.

—Right.

—You are a brave fellow.

—Thank you, Martha.

—It's like opening a valve.

—Is what?

—I feel like I'm feeding off the atmosphere and the skin of the earth coming through me and down the drain and down into the earth again.

—What is the valve here?

—My mouth. I've stopped eating and drinking.

—It's not allowed.

—Fuck that. I'll fast for a day.

—Viewers think I'm screwing you.

—They can think what they want. Of course, they're not exactly thinking, are they?

—They are not.

—It's more like clack-clackety-clack.

—In addition to that, I am tired of the reproductive process.

—They're like ducks. Quack, quack.

—Okay. We need to decide. Evade persecution. The mountains perhaps.

—No.

—What then?

—Let's fight back. Call a hearing. You're entitled to a show. Am I right?

—You are.

—Let's give them a run for their money. I have a secret which is—my favorite boy was Jimmy Dark. Sweet and vulnerable and terrified.

Tell that to the Committee—you see that we don't have much more to do, Jim. Keep your hat on.

*

—Remember I have a superior.

—Who is he? I'll tell you—he is interested in what his body gives off—his ears and his mouth and his sweat and his nose material and his armpits and his emotions. His faulty emanations. Doctor Dee. In private sitting around or watching TV.

—He's a G-d guy, we're working for the good of G-d.

—You can handle it.

—I'm no good being swept up by G-d. I mean what is that? I need to function like a man with a job, a man with a job to do.

—Stop doing that. You can't keep doing that.

—What?

—Stop doing it. Your hands are moving.

—Thank you.

—There's a woman floating around in the atmospheres high up in a balloon.

—Who is she?

—Don't know. She emerged on the screen day before yesterday. She's dropping mud bombs.

—Shoot her down of course.

—Of course.

—Whack her out of there and clear the flyways.

—Will do, Martha.

—Stop.

—What?

—The jiggling of your hands. It's driving me nuts. Stop it.

—You've heard of the Woman in the mountain, a thousand tentacles and five hundred mouths, a hundred eyes, of course.

—No.

—She eats lies.

—Don't tell me.

—Static.

—Ah.

—She sneaks in there and causes static.

—Let's get organized.

—Get up there with two-thousand-pound bunker bombs.

—Okay, Jim.

—Smithereens.

—Time to organize, name our people.

—Martha had some clues.

—You all right, Jim?

—Definitely, Dr. Dee.

—Avoid chaos.

—Of course.

—Factions appear. It's only normal. You must take a stand.

—Right.

—And at the same time hang onto power. Be brash have attitude. Look good on the screen.

—Now the Judge is down the laws are prickly.

—What do you mean?

—I might make a move. I might do a sideways two-step.

—Drop the charges and it goes away.

—I think it's a good move, drop charges and get out of the way.

—So do I.

—So do I what?

—I understand your point of view, and where you're going with this.

—I'm not going anywhere.

—His reputation is ruined in any event. Old Jim.

—People get out there and grab it, get famous and make money.

—Entertainment has a value.

—What I'm saying. Here's Martha: It's a November afternoon in the city. The dryer in the garage thrums, cars go by. The maid makes incongruous noise in another room.

—Continue.

—He died right there in the hall; he was trying to put his pants on.

—No. He took a twelve-gauge to his mouth. Blew his brains out.

—Well. It depends on how you see things. We're not all of the same mind.

—There's an insurance issue and a criminal issue here.

—Let's get this straight. He just died. Nobody killed him, nobody cried, he just died.

—That's not what I heard.

—What did you hear?

—He went on a rally tour and busted his chops. Tongue out, eyes bulged, hair fell out, veins popped, and he dropped dead right there on stage, a hundred people clapping their hands. They applauded as he stood there dead. An ambulance came and they chanted his name. The President's. We don't speak his name no more out of decency and respect.

—And the Wilsons?

—I have not forgot the Wilsons. They are hunkered down in Middletown.

—Oh, for G-d's sake.

—What?

—The inveterate rhyming. What's wrong with you?

—I had wonderful teachers in English class.

—Okay.

—Fine men who toed the line.

—I'm talking flesh and blood right now, not English bullshit. Blood and entrails and brains.

—Right.

—Set up a shoot and we'll take care of business.

—Will do.

—Use good people, ones who won't faint or lose their bowels. This country is going to the dogs.

*

—Your Uncle John?

—Signals me.

—How so?

—By how much he leaves on his plate. Yes or no. Go or stay.

—You'll be offstage as it were, off screen as well.

—That's the deal.

—And then you run.

—Then I run. And I have a mile head start.

—That so?

—It's in the books.

—Will you regret your life?

—No.

—Remorse?

—No, I enjoyed myself in hell. Hard to do, eh? I enjoyed my body to its full and I kept it pure as heaven, whatever people mumble in the dark of their stupidity and their cowardice. Creepy minds scuttling about or glued to their screens.

—We are not mountebanks like you and your family. And now what will they do under the circumstances?

—They'll disperse. The mountains and the sea. I to a forest glen.

—Somewhere the grinding of a motor endlessly grinding and a plane in the sky roaring.

—Okay.

—Looks like rain to me I can smell it.

—Okay.

—And the quest. Let's get down to it.

—Setting the scene. Late afternoon in the city. Longing for rain.

—Okay.

—We attacked in force and the line of force concludes the issue.

—Wait a minute.

—What?

—What did you say? I have no idea what you're talking about.

—What?

—You said "quest."

—You are one dumb fuck. You must think Jews have artillery on the moon.

—I do not.

—Aimed our way.

—No, but you must keep an eye out.

—Start looking for a job. On a farm maybe.

—Yes, sir.

—Onward.

—The Wilsons put up a fight in the court of public opinion.

—The verdict?

—Sarah gets to make a run for it. The family will receive boats and camping equipment. Funds to be verified by the Jury.

—A catastrophe for Jimmy Dark. And Martha?

—Someone in her camp denounced her.

—Jealousy no doubt.

—No doubt.

—Dolores.

—A co-conspirator.

—Sadly, sadly.

—Made an entire B-movie out of it, a noir, double crosses, fake identity, the lot.

—The Viewers will do that sort of thing, spread lies and back stab. I remember one fellow in the department. Like Jimmy. Thought he was smarter than everyone else.

—We can't have that.

—Henpecked fellow. His family were high-end producers.

—We hung him in the plaza at dawn. Left the Camera on him for twenty-four hours.

—I remember. Do it for Dolores, too.

—It's done. We buried her alive on the high plains. Camera there for the end.

—You know, the things people will do on TV. It's astonishing.

—You can't be sure of the species anymore.

—I didn't expect a thunderclap, an earthquake, or hurricane when Jimbo died, but I thought a proper mourning was his due. He gave his life for this society.

—What did he do?

—Come on. He kept the streets clean. He enforced the law. What more do you want from a person? Today? He had his faults. Perhaps I over-bearded him. Made demands. He tried. Kept his dignity. Was able to stand there as I yelled. Kept his composure. Just barely. We went for counseling, and he cried for an hour. One hour straight. No pause.

—What will you do now, Martha?

—And his endlessly moving hands.

—What will you do?

—I'll stay on. I'll maintain. I have my slots, my social media, and I'll make an appearance here and there. And I'll keep an eye out. People who sneak in. People who don't belong, like the Wilsons. Others. We've only cracked the nut. There's more to go. Meat and bones. Concentration camps. Wire.

—Thank you.

—You bet.

—Thank you.

—The time will come, you know, high walls and machine guns. Arrows. Viruses and war. A higher vigilance for all.

—Thanks, again.

—No problem. Live long and prosper.

*

—Let's go my dear, the hounds are howling.

END

Murray Mednick is the founder of the Padua Hills Playwrights Festival and Workshop, where he served as Artistic Director from 1978 through 1995. Born in Brooklyn, New York, in 1939, he was for many years a playwright-in-residence at New York's Theatre Genesis, a seminal group in the development of Off-Off Broadway. He is the recipient of two Rockefeller Foundation grants, a Guggenheim Fellowship, an OBIE, several Bay Area Critics Awards, a 1992 Ovation Lifetime Achievement Award from Theatre LA for outstanding contributions to Los Angeles theater. Mednick was awarded the 2002 Margaret Harford Award for Sustained Excellence in Theater by the Los Angeles Drama Critics Circle, and a lifetime achievement award from *L.A. Weekly.*

Also available from Padua Playwrights Press:

Outlaw Theatre: Field Notes from the Padua Hills Playwrights Workshop and Festival (2022)
Essays by Migdalia Cruz, Martin Epstein, Anne Garcia-Romero, David Henry Hwang, Leon Martell, Murray Mednick, Marlane Meyer, Susan Mosakowski, John O'Keefe, Gray Palmer, Beth Ruscio, Peter Stathis, John Steppling, Wes Walker, Guy Zimmerman

Mayakovsky and Stalin (2020)
Murray Mednick

Villon (2016)
Murray Mednick

I Might Be the Person You Are Talking To: Short Plays from Twenty Cutting-edge Los Angeles Playwrights (2015)
Works by Sissy Boyd, Hank Bunker, Heidi Darchuk, Juli Crockett Feldman, Susan Hayden, Coleman Hough, Bernard Goldberg, Michael Hacker, Rachel Jendrzejewski, Marc Jensen, Christopher Kelley, Murray Mednick, Kevin O'Sullivan, Gray Palmer, Chris Rossi, April Rouveyrol, Cheryl Slean, Wesley Walker, Sharon Yablon, and Guy Zimmerman.

Fever Dreams: Recent Work from Padua (2012)
Works by Sissy Boyd, Hank Bunker, Heidi Darchuk, Murray Mednick, John Steppling, Rita Valencia, Sharon Yablon, and Guy Zimmerman

Beneath the Dusty Trees: The Gary Plays, an Octet (2012)
Murray Mednick

Hipsters in Distress: Are You Lookin? and Other Plays (2005)
by Murray Mednick

Plays for a New Millennium: New Work from Padua (2004)
Works by Neena Beber, María Irene Fornés, Murray Mednick, John O'Keefe, John Steppling, Wesley Walker, Guy Zimmerman

Padua: Plays from the Padua Hills Playwrights Festival (2003)
Works by Neena Beber, María Irene Fornés, Joe Goodrich, Murray Mednick, Marlane Meyer, Susan Mosakowski, John O 'Keefe, John Steppling, and Kelly Stuart.

Three Plays by Murray Mednick (2003)